First World War
and Army of Occupation
War Diary
France, Belgium and Germany

32 DIVISION
97 Infantry Brigade
Border Regiment
11th Battalion
22 November 1915 - 16 July 1918

WO95/2403/1

The Naval & Military Press Ltd
www.nmarchive.com
Published in association with The National Archives

Published by

The Naval & Military Press Ltd

Unit 10 Ridgewood Industrial Park,

Uckfield, East Sussex,

TN22 5QE England

Tel: +44 (0) 1825 749494

www.naval-military-press.com

www.nmarchive.com

This diary has been reprinted in facsimile from the original. Any imperfections are inevitably reproduced and the quality may fall short of modern type and cartographic standards.

© **Crown Copyright**
Images reproduced by permission of The National Archives, London, England, 2015.

Contents

Document type	Place/Title	Date From	Date To
Heading	WO95/2403-1 97 Bde 11 Bttn. Border Regt.		
Heading	32nd Division 97th Infy Bde 11th Bn Border Regt Nov 1915-Jly 1918 Disbanded.		
Heading	32nd Div. 11th Border Regt. Vol:I Nov & Dec'15.		
War Diary	Codford	22/11/1915	23/11/1915
War Diary	Boulogne	24/11/1915	24/11/1915
War Diary	Gorenflos	25/11/1915	26/11/1915
War Diary	Picquigny	27/11/1915	27/11/1915
War Diary	Villers Bocage.	28/11/1915	01/12/1915
War Diary	Molliens Au Bois	02/12/1915	11/12/1915
War Diary	Bouzincourt	12/12/1915	18/12/1915
War Diary	F.1 Sub-Sector.	19/12/1915	23/12/1915
War Diary	Bouzincourt	24/12/1915	26/12/1915
War Diary	F.1. Sub Sector	27/12/1915	31/12/1915
Heading	11th Borders Regt. Vol 2 Fail		
War Diary	Aveluy	01/01/1916	06/01/1916
War Diary	F1 Sector	07/01/1916	13/01/1916
War Diary	F1 Sub-Sector	14/01/1916	14/01/1916
War Diary	Bouzincourt.	15/01/1916	20/01/1916
War Diary	F1 Sub Sector	21/01/1916	25/01/1916
War Diary	F1. Sector.	26/01/1916	28/01/1916
War Diary	Aveluy	29/01/1916	31/01/1916
Heading	97th Brigade. 32nd Division. 11th Battalion. The Border Regiment February 1916		
Heading	32 11th Border Regt. Vol:3		
War Diary	Aveluy	01/02/1916	04/02/1916
War Diary	F1 Sector	05/02/1916	10/02/1916
War Diary	Albert	11/02/1916	16/02/1916
War Diary	Hemencourt	17/02/1916	23/02/1916
War Diary	Millencourt	24/02/1916	29/02/1916
Heading	11th Badey Vol 4		
War Diary	Henencourt	01/03/1916	01/03/1916
War Diary	E I Sector	02/03/1916	10/03/1916
War Diary	Albert	11/03/1916	16/03/1916
War Diary	E I Sector	17/03/1916	22/03/1916
War Diary	Dernancourt	23/03/1916	28/03/1916
War Diary	E I Sector.	29/03/1916	31/03/1916
Heading	97th Brigade. 32nd Division. 11th Battalion The Border Regiment. April 1916.		
War Diary	E I Sector	01/04/1916	03/04/1916
War Diary	Senlis	04/04/1916	11/04/1916
War Diary	Aveluy	12/04/1916	16/04/1916
War Diary	Contay Wood	17/04/1916	17/05/1916
War Diary	Authville Sector	18/05/1916	18/05/1916
War Diary	Authville	19/05/1916	21/05/1916
War Diary	Croeifix Corner	22/05/1916	25/05/1916
War Diary	Authville Sector	26/05/1916	29/05/1916
War Diary	Bouzincourt	30/05/1916	31/05/1916
Heading	97th Brigade. 32nd Division. 1/11th Battalion The Border Regiment June 1916		

War Diary	Bouzincourt	01/06/1916	05/06/1916
War Diary	Senlis	06/06/1916	11/06/1916
War Diary	Contay	12/06/1916	22/06/1916
War Diary	Authville Sector	23/06/1916	26/06/1916
War Diary	Crucifix Corner	27/06/1916	30/06/1916
Heading	97th Inf. Bde. 32nd Div. War Diary 11th Battn. The Border Regiment. July 1916.		
War Diary	Authville Wood	01/07/1916	03/07/1916
War Diary	Crucifix	04/07/1916	04/07/1916
War Diary	Crucifix Corner	04/07/1916	04/07/1916
War Diary	Contay Wood	05/07/1916	07/07/1916
War Diary	Senlis	08/07/1916	08/07/1916
War Diary	F1 Sub Sector	09/07/1916	11/07/1916
War Diary	Crucifix Corner	12/07/1916	15/07/1916
War Diary	Bougencourt	16/07/1916	17/07/1916
War Diary	Sus St Leger	18/07/1916	21/07/1916
War Diary	Allouagne	22/07/1916	26/07/1916
War Diary	Bethune	27/07/1916	29/07/1916
War Diary	Noyelles	30/07/1916	31/07/1916
Heading	97th Brigade. 32nd Division. 11th Battalion The Border Regiment August 1916		
Heading	War Diary of 11th Border Regiment from 1st August 1916 to 31st August 1916 (Volume 9)		
Miscellaneous			
War Diary	Noyelle	01/08/1916	04/08/1916
War Diary	Cambrin Sector	05/08/1916	09/08/1916
War Diary	Front Line Trs (Railway Keep) Battn. H.Q.	10/08/1916	13/08/1916
War Diary	Annequin (Reserve)	14/08/1916	16/08/1916
War Diary	Cambrin Sector (Front Line Trs) Railway Keep (Battn. H.Q)	17/08/1916	20/08/1916
War Diary	Bethune	21/08/1916	22/08/1916
War Diary	Philosophe	23/08/1916	23/08/1916
War Diary	(Support Tr) Hulluch Sector	24/08/1916	27/08/1916
War Diary	Front Line Trenches (Hulluch Sector)	28/08/1916	30/08/1916
War Diary	Bethune	31/08/1916	31/08/1916
Heading	97th Brigade. 32nd Division. 11th Battalion The Border Regiment September 1916		
Heading	War Diary of 11th Border Regt. from 1st September, 1916 to 30th September, 1916. Volume 10.		
War Diary	Bethune	01/09/1916	07/09/1916
War Diary	Reserve Billets at Quenoy. (Cuinchy Sector)	08/09/1916	11/09/1916
War Diary	Front Line Trs Cuinchy Sector	12/09/1916	15/09/1916
War Diary	Reserve Line (Harley Street) (Billets)	15/09/1916	19/09/1916
War Diary	Front Line Trenches Coinchy Sector.	20/09/1916	23/09/1916
War Diary	Le. Quesnoy (Reserve)	24/09/1916	25/09/1916
War Diary	Annezin	26/09/1916	30/09/1916
Heading	97th Brigade. 32nd Division. 11th Battalion The Border Regiment October 1916		
Heading	War Diary of 11th Border Regiment from 1st October 1916 to 31st October 1916 (Volume 11)		
War Diary	Annezin	01/10/1916	03/10/1916
War Diary	Cambrin Sector (Front Line Trs)	04/10/1916	07/10/1916
War Diary	Cambrin Sector (Support Line)	08/10/1916	10/10/1916
War Diary	Cambrin Sector	11/10/1916	13/10/1916
War Diary	Bethune	14/10/1916	14/10/1916
War Diary	Labeuvriere	15/10/1916	15/10/1916

War Diary	Monchy Breton	16/10/1916	16/10/1916
War Diary	Moncheaux	17/10/1916	17/10/1916
War Diary	Longuevillete	18/10/1916	20/10/1916
War Diary	Herissat.	21/10/1916	22/10/1916
War Diary	Bouzincourt	23/10/1916	29/10/1916
War Diary	Herissat	30/10/1916	30/10/1916
War Diary	La Vilogne	31/10/1916	31/10/1916
Heading	97th Brigade. 32nd Division. 11th Battalion The Border Regiment November 1916		
Heading	War Diary of 11th Border Regiment from 1/11/16 to 30/11/16. (Volume 12)		
Miscellaneous			
War Diary	La Vilogne	01/11/1916	12/11/1916
War Diary	Contay	13/11/1916	13/11/1916
War Diary	Black Horse Bridge.	14/11/1916	14/11/1916
War Diary	Englebelmer	15/11/1916	16/11/1916
War Diary	Trenches Redan Sector	17/11/1916	17/11/1916
War Diary	Wagon Road	18/11/1916	19/11/1916
War Diary	Mailly Maillet	20/11/1916	22/11/1916
War Diary	Arqueves	23/11/1916	24/11/1916
War Diary	Gezaincourt	25/11/1916	25/11/1916
War Diary	Berteaucourt	26/11/1916	30/11/1916
Heading	War Diary of 11th Border Regiment from 1st December 1916 to 31st December 1916 (Volume 13)		
Miscellaneous			
War Diary	Berteaucourt	01/12/1916	16/12/1916
War Diary	Pushvillers	17/12/1916	06/01/1917
War Diary	Corcelles	07/01/1917	10/01/1917
War Diary	Trenches Sub-Sector C.3	11/01/1917	11/01/1917
War Diary	Corcelles	12/01/1917	13/01/1917
War Diary	Bus	14/01/1917	17/01/1917
War Diary	Mailly Mallet.	18/01/1917	23/01/1917
War Diary	Lythan Camp	24/01/1917	26/01/1917
War Diary	Sector R 2.	27/01/1917	28/01/1917
War Diary	Beaumont Hamel	29/01/1917	30/01/1917
War Diary	R 1 Sector	31/01/1917	31/01/1917
Miscellaneous			
Heading	War Diary of 11th Border Regt. from 1st Jan to 31st Jan 1917. (Volume 14)		
Heading	War Diary of 11th Border Regiment from 1st February 1917 to 28th February 1917. (Volume 15)		
Miscellaneous			
War Diary	Sub Sector R.I	01/02/1917	02/02/1917
War Diary	Beaumont Hamel.	01/02/1917	02/02/1917
War Diary	Lythan Camp (Beaussart).	03/02/1917	09/02/1917
War Diary	R.1.a.5.5 Sub Sector R.1. Beaumont Hamel.	10/02/1917	10/02/1917
War Diary	R.1.a.5.5	10/02/1917	10/02/1917
War Diary	R.1.a.5.5 Sub Sector R.1. Beaumont Hamel	11/02/1917	11/02/1917
War Diary	R.1.a.5.5.	11/02/1917	11/02/1917
War Diary	R.1.a.5.5 Sub Sector R1 Beaumont Hamel.	11/02/1917	12/02/1917
War Diary	Beaumont Hamel	12/02/1917	14/02/1917
War Diary	Acheux	15/02/1917	17/02/1917
War Diary	Mirvaux	18/02/1917	20/02/1917
War Diary	Camon Near Amien	21/02/1917	22/02/1917
War Diary	Weincourt	23/02/1917	25/02/1917
War Diary	Quesnel	25/02/1917	28/02/1917

Heading	War Diary of 11th Border Regiment. From 1st March 1917 to 31st March 1917 (Volume 16)		
Miscellaneous			
War Diary	Le Quesnel	01/03/1917	01/03/1917
War Diary	Kuropatkin	01/03/1917	04/03/1917
War Diary	Ney Sector Opposite Fouquerscourt.	05/03/1917	08/03/1917
War Diary	Kuropatkin.	09/03/1917	11/03/1917
War Diary	Ney Sector.	11/03/1917	14/03/1917
War Diary	Le Quesnel	15/03/1917	16/03/1917
War Diary	Rouvroy.	17/03/1917	17/03/1917
War Diary	Hattencourt.	18/03/1917	18/03/1917
War Diary	Herley	19/03/1917	19/03/1917
War Diary	Nesle.	20/03/1917	27/03/1917
War Diary	Foreste.	28/03/1917	31/03/1917
Heading	War Diary of 11th Border Regiment From 1st April 1917 to 30th April 1917. (Volume 17)		
Miscellaneous			
War Diary	Savy	01/04/1917	06/04/1917
War Diary	Holnon	07/04/1917	14/04/1917
War Diary	N. of Fayet.	14/04/1917	15/04/1917
War Diary	Germaine	16/04/1917	19/04/1917
War Diary	Hombleux	20/04/1917	23/04/1917
War Diary	Offoy	24/04/1917	30/04/1917
Heading	War Diary of 11th Border Regiment from 1st May 1917 to 31st May 1917 (Volume 18).		
Miscellaneous			
War Diary	Offoy	01/05/1917	14/05/1917
War Diary	Puzeaux	15/05/1917	15/05/1917
War Diary	Caix	16/05/1917	16/05/1917
War Diary	Domart S/La Luce	17/05/1917	17/05/1917
War Diary	Domart	18/05/1917	25/05/1917
War Diary	Domart S/Luce	26/05/1917	26/05/1917
War Diary	Domart	27/05/1917	29/05/1917
War Diary	Villers Bretonneux	30/05/1917	31/05/1917
Heading	War Diary of 11th Border Regiment from 1st June 1917 to 30th June 1917 (Volume 19).		
Miscellaneous			
War Diary	Villers-Brettoneux	01/06/1917	01/06/1917
War Diary	Neuf-Berquin	02/06/1917	14/06/1917
War Diary	Godewaersveldt	15/06/1917	16/06/1917
War Diary	St Pol S/M	17/06/1917	18/06/1917
War Diary	Coxyde	19/06/1917	19/06/1917
War Diary	Ooste-Dunkerque	20/06/1917	30/06/1917
Heading	War Diary of the 11th Battn. The Border Regt. 1st to 31st July 1917 Vol 20		
Heading	War Diary of 11th Border Regiment From 1st July 1917 to 31st July 1917. (Volume 20)		
Miscellaneous			
War Diary	Vieuport-Lombartzyde Sector	01/07/1917	05/07/1917
War Diary	Nieuport	05/07/1917	09/07/1917
War Diary	Nieuport S.W of Lombartzyde	10/07/1917	10/07/1917
War Diary	Line. S.W of Lombartzyde	10/07/1917	11/07/1917
War Diary	Nieuport	11/07/1917	11/07/1917
War Diary	Coxyde	12/07/1917	15/07/1917
War Diary	Ghyuelde	16/07/1917	19/07/1917
War Diary	Bray-Dunes	20/07/1917	25/07/1917

War Diary	Coxyde	26/07/1917	31/07/1917
Heading	War Diary of 11th Borders Regiment From 1st August to 31st August (Volume No. 21)		
War Diary	Coxyde	01/08/1917	13/08/1917
War Diary	Oost-Dunkerque	14/08/1917	14/08/1917
War Diary	Bray-Dunes	15/08/1917	27/08/1917
War Diary	Canada Camp	28/08/1917	28/08/1917
War Diary	Oost Dunkerque	29/08/1917	31/08/1917
Heading	War Diary of 11th Border Regiment From 1st September 1917 to 30th September 1917 (Volume 22)		
Miscellaneous			
War Diary	Oost-Dunkerque	01/09/1917	03/09/1917
War Diary	In the Line	04/09/1917	10/09/1917
War Diary	Nulpen	11/09/1917	15/09/1917
War Diary	In the line	16/09/1917	20/09/1917
War Diary	Coxyde	21/09/1917	21/09/1917
War Diary	La Panne	22/09/1917	22/09/1917
War Diary	Zudycoote	23/09/1917	24/09/1917
War Diary	La Panne	25/09/1917	28/09/1917
War Diary	In the Line	29/09/1917	30/09/1917
Heading	War Diary of 11th Border Regiment 1st to 31st October 1917 (Volume No. 23)		
Miscellaneous			
War Diary	In the Line	01/10/1917	05/10/1917
War Diary	Coxyde	06/10/1917	06/10/1917
War Diary	Teteghem	09/10/1917	24/10/1917
War Diary	Zegers Cappel	25/10/1917	25/10/1917
War Diary	Foubrouck Area	26/10/1917	31/10/1917
Heading	War Diary of 11th Border Regiment From 1st to 30th November, 1917 (Volume No. 24)		
Miscellaneous			
War Diary	Rubrouck Area	01/11/1917	10/11/1917
War Diary	Winnezeele Area	11/11/1917	11/11/1917
War Diary	Road Camp	12/11/1917	21/11/1917
War Diary	Hilltop Farm	23/11/1917	23/11/1917
War Diary	Bellevue Area	24/11/1917	25/11/1917
War Diary	Westroosebeeke	26/11/1917	26/11/1917
War Diary	Left Sub-Sector	27/11/1917	27/11/1917
War Diary	Hill Top Farm	28/11/1917	29/11/1917
War Diary	Wurst Farm	30/11/1917	30/11/1917
Heading	War Diary of 11th Border Regiment From 1st to 31st December 1917 (Volume No. 25)		
Miscellaneous			
War Diary	Westroosebeek Area	02/12/1917	03/12/1917
War Diary	Brake Camp	04/02/1917	04/02/1917
War Diary	Damere Area	04/12/1917	04/12/1917
War Diary	Brake Camp	05/12/1917	08/12/1917
War Diary	Dambre Camp	09/12/1917	17/12/1917
War Diary	Wurst Farm	18/12/1917	20/12/1917
War Diary	In the Line	21/12/1917	23/12/1917
War Diary	Siege Camp	24/12/1917	30/12/1917
War Diary	Tournehem	31/12/1917	31/12/1917
Heading	War Diary of 11th Border Regiment From 1st to 31st January 1918. (Volume No. 26)		
Miscellaneous			
War Diary	Tournehem	01/01/1918	20/01/1918

War Diary	Caribou Camp	21/01/1918	25/01/1918
War Diary	La Bergerie Camp	26/01/1918	27/01/1918
War Diary	In The Line	28/01/1918	31/01/1918
Heading	War Diary of 11th Border Regt. 1st Feb 1918-28th Feb 1918 Volume 25.		
Miscellaneous			
War Diary	In the Field	01/02/1918	01/02/1918
War Diary	Bosinqe	02/02/1918	04/02/1918
War Diary	In the Field	05/02/1918	08/02/1918
War Diary	In the Field Buche X Rds.	09/02/1918	18/02/1918
War Diary	Woeston	19/02/1918	28/02/1918
War Diary	Woeston (Vandamme Camp).	01/03/1918	03/03/1918
War Diary	In the Line	04/03/1918	11/03/1918
War Diary	In the Line	10/03/1918	14/03/1918
War Diary	Bde Reserve	14/03/1918	18/03/1918
War Diary	In the Line	18/03/1918	21/03/1918
War Diary	Div. Res.	22/03/1918	22/03/1918
War Diary	Canal Bank.	22/03/1918	25/03/1918
War Diary	Wanquetin	26/03/1918	26/03/1918
War Diary	Ransart	27/03/1918	27/03/1918
War Diary	In the Field	28/03/1918	31/03/1918
War Diary	In the Line X.25.d.9.1 & X.27.a.0.0	01/04/1918	04/04/1918
War Diary	Purple Line	04/04/1918	06/04/1918
War Diary	Purple Line.	07/04/1918	07/04/1918
War Diary	In the Line F.6.a.4.5 to S.25.d.9.1	08/04/1918	12/04/1918
War Diary	In the Line	12/04/1918	17/04/1918
War Diary	Bde Res.	17/04/1918	21/04/1918
War Diary	In the Line	21/04/1918	26/04/1918
War Diary	Lahertie	26/04/1918	30/04/1918
Heading	Appendices.		
Miscellaneous	Instruction for 97th Infantry Brigade when in Reserve.	25/04/1918	25/04/1918
Miscellaneous	A B C D		
Miscellaneous	Action		
Miscellaneous			
Miscellaneous	11th Border Regt.	25/04/1918	25/04/1918
Miscellaneous	To 97th Inf Bde.	27/04/1918	27/04/1918
Miscellaneous	11th Border Regt.	30/04/1918	30/04/1918
Heading	War Diary of 11th Border Regt. From May 1st 1918 To May 31st Volume 33		
War Diary	Laherliere	01/05/1918	03/05/1918
War Diary	Berles-Au-Bois	03/05/1918	09/05/1918
War Diary	Larbret	12/05/1918	19/05/1918
War Diary		13/05/1918	30/05/1918
Heading	War Diary of 11th Border Regt. From:- June 1st 1918 To:- June 30th 1918. Vol No. 34		
War Diary		01/06/1918	16/06/1918
War Diary	Pende	16/06/1918	29/06/1918
War Diary		05/06/1918	16/06/1918
War Diary	Pende	16/06/1918	29/06/1918
Heading	War Diary of 11th Battn. Border Regt. From:- 1st July 1918 To:- 31st July 1918. Volume		
War Diary	Ailly Le Haut Clocher	01/07/1918	20/07/1918
War Diary	Epagne	21/07/1918	22/07/1918
War Diary	Abancourt	23/07/1918	31/07/1918
War Diary	C.R. S/9084 Appendix I	16/07/1918	16/07/1918

W0095/24031
an Roe
11 Kth Booger Peen

32ND DIVISION
97TH INFY BDE

11TH BN BORDER REGT

NOV 1915 – JLY 1918

DISBANDED

11th Border Regt.
Vol: I

1928
F/

33rd Div

No regts

Suidele I.P.
7 sheets

11th Border Regt

WAR DIARY
INTELLIGENCE SUMMARY
(Erase heading not required.)

Army Form C. 2118.

Instructions regarding War Diaries and Intelligence Summaries are contained in F. S. Regs., Part II and the Staff Manual respectively. Title pages will be prepared in manuscript.

Hour, Date, Place		Summary of Events and Information	Remarks and references to Appendices
2/11/15	CODFORD.	Transport and baggage with 2 Officers and 101 other ranks proceeded under Major P.G.W. DIGGLE to HAVRE.	
3/11/15	"	Battalion proceeded in two trains to FOLKESTONE, for BOULOGNE, strength 23 Officers 896 Other Ranks.	
4/11/15	BOULOGNE.	At BOULOGNE, leaving 4.5pm by train for LONG PRÉ.	Capt. L.B HOGARTH and 3 Other Ranks left sick in hospital at BOULOGNE. Interpreter attached.
5/11/15	GORENFLOS	Marched from LONG PRÉ at 1.0 am, arrived GORENFLOS 7.30 am – billets.	
"	"		
6/11/15	PICQUIGNY	Marched to PICQUIGNY, arriving there 1-30 pm. – billets.	2/Lt. J.W. MOORE and batman rejoined. This Officer had proceeded via HAVRE for disembarkation duties 19/11/15
7/11/15	VILLERS BOCAGE.	Marched to VILLERS BOCAGE – billets.	
8/11/15	"	Close Order Drill.	

WAR DIARY
INTELLIGENCE SUMMARY
(Erase heading not required.)

Army Form C. 2118.

Instructions regarding War Diaries and Intelligence Summaries are contained in F. S. Regs., Part II and the Staff Manual respectively. Title pages will be prepared in manuscript.

Hour, Date, Place		Summary of Events and Information	Remarks and references to Appendices
30/11/15	VILLERS BOCAGE	Short Route March, and Inspections –	
1/12/15.	"	"	
2/12/15	MOLLIENS AU BOIS	Marched to MOLLIENS AU BOIS, arrived 12.30pm – billets.	
3/12/15	"	⎫ Battalion unable to do much work on account of	
4/12/15	"	⎬ very wet weather. Inspection, lectures, Physical Exercises.	
5/12/15	"	⎭	
6/12/15	"	⎫ 8 men per platoon practised in the use of live hand	
7/12/15	"	⎬ Grenades under instruction of Lieut Kemp of MANCHESTER	
8/12/15	"	⎭ REGIMENT	
9/12/15	"	Remainder of the Battalion was occupied with Inspections,	
10/12/15	"	close order drill and short route marches.	

WAR DIARY
INTELLIGENCE SUMMARY

Army Form C. 2118.

(Erase heading not required.)

Hour, Date, Place	Summary of Events and Information	Remarks and references to Appendices
/12/15 BOUZINCOURT	Left half Battalion under Major P.G.W. DIGGLE proceeded to camp at MILLENCOURT. Right half Battalion with Headquarters and Transport proceeded to Camp at BOUZINCOURT. Officers and N.C.O.s right half Battalion, having been conveyed by motor bus from MOLLIENS AU BOIS, were attached for instruction in the trenches to garrison of F.1 & F.2. Sub-Sector.	
13/12/15 "	Four platoons right half Battalion attached for instruction in the trenches to garrison of F.1. Sub-Sector. Four platoons right half Battalion attached for instruction in the trenches to garrison of F.2. Sub-Sector.	One Other Rank wounded.
14/12/15 "	Right half Battalion returned to BOUZINCOURT. Officers and N.C.O.s left half Battalion attached for instruction in the trenches to garrison of F.1 & F.2. Sub-Sectors.	One Other Rank wounded, & died 14/12/15.

Army Form C. 2118.

WAR DIARY

INTELLIGENCE SUMMARY.

(Erase heading not required.)

Instructions regarding War Diaries and Intelligence
Summaries are contained in F. S. Regs., Part II
and the Staff Manual respectively. Title pages
will be prepared in manuscript.

Hour, Date, Place		Summary of Events and Information	Remarks and references to Appendices
15/12/15	BOUZINCOURT	Four platoons of Left Half Battalion attached for instructions in the trenches to garrison of F.1. sub-sector.	Two Other Ranks wounded. Capt. L.R. HOGARTH attached for duty to C.R.E. 51st Division.
16/12/15	"	Four platoons of Left Half Battalion attached for instruction in the trenches to garrison of F.2. sub-sector. Left half Battalion returned to MILLENCOURT.	
17/12/15	"	Right half Battalion relieved 2 Companies of garrison of F.1. sub-sector.	
18/12/15	"	Left half Battalion relieved 2 Companies of garrison of F.2. sub-sector.	
19/12/15	F.1. Sub-Sector	Battalion took over F.1. Sub-Sector from 1/6th Argyle and Sutherland Highlanders.	One Other Rank sent to Base for dental treatment.
20/12/15	" "		One Other Rank wounded.
21/12/15	" "		—
22/12/15	" "		Capt. C. CLARK. O.C. B Company admitted to hospital. Capt. B.C. HARRISON took over command of B. Company.

(7.3989) W4141—463. 400,000. 9/14. H.&J.Ltd. Forms/C. 2118/10.

Army Form C. 2118.

WAR DIARY

(Erase heading not required.)

Instructions regarding War Diaries and Intelligence Summaries are contained in F.S. Regs., Part II and the Staff Manual respectively. Title pages will be prepared in manuscript.

Hour, Date, Place		Summary of Events and Information	Remarks and references to Appendices
3/12/15	F.I. SUB SECTOR	Battalion relieved by 19th H.L.I. and proceeded to camp at BOUZINCOURT.	
4/12/15	BOUZINCOURT	1 Officer & 50 Other Ranks fatigue to R.E. for erecting huts. Remainder Battalion cleaning Rifles and Equipment.	
5/12/15	"	Church Parade. "A" Company proceeded to AVELUY. accommodated in billets to find guards, fatigues etc for 97th BRIGADE HQRS.	
6/12/15	"	"	
7/12/15	F.I. SUB SECTOR	Relieved 19th H.L.I. in F.I. SUB-SECTOR.	One Other Rank wounded.
8/12/15	"	No unusual occurrence to report. Special attention was paid to the repairing of trenches and construction of dug-outs.	
9/12/15	"	"	One Other Rank wounded
10/12/15	"	"	One Other Rank sustained self inflicted wound in the foot. Court of Enquiry finding "accidental".
11/12/15	"	Relieved by 19th H.L.I. Battalion proceeded to AVELUY billets.	

11th Border Rgt.
Vol 2

11TH BORDER REGT.
WAR DIARY
or
INTELLIGENCE SUMMARY
(Erase heading not required.)

Army Form C. 2118.

Instructions regarding War Diaries and Intelligence Summaries are contained in F.S. Regs., Part II and the Staff Manual respectively. Title pages will be prepared in manuscript.

Hour, Date, Place	Summary of Events and Information	Remarks and references to Appendices
AVELUY. 1/1/16	⎫	
" 2/1/16	⎪	
" 3/1/16	⎬ R.E. Fatigues.	
" 4/1/16	⎪	
" 5/1/16	⎪	
" 6/1/16	⎭	
F1 Sector 7/1/16	11TH BORDER REGT relieved 17TH M.L.I. in F1 Sector. Casualty 1 man wounded	Batt on Right 8TH NORFOLKS. Batt on Left. 2ND KOYLI.
F1 Sector 8/1/16	Day quiet	
F1 Sector 9/1/16	"	
F1 Sector 10/1/16	"	
F1 Sector 11/1/16	Casualty. 1 man wounded.	
F1 Sector 12/1/16	Day quiet	
F1 Sector 13/1/16	Casualty 1 man wounded.	

11TH BORDER REGT
WAR DIARY
or
INTELLIGENCE SUMMARY.
(Erase heading not required.)

Army Form C. 2118.

Instructions regarding War Diaries and Intelligence Summaries are contained in F.S. Regs., Part II and the Staff Manual respectively. Title pages will be prepared in manuscript.

Hour, Date, Place		Summary of Events and Information	Remarks and references to Appendices
F. Sub-rector	14/1/16	Front quiet. The 17TH H.L.I. relieved the Border Regt. Border Regt returned to rear billets at BOUZINCOURT	C. Coy. Border Regt. Rest billets at AVELUY.
BOUZINCOURT	15/1/16	} Battalion in rest billets at BOUZINCOURT	
"	16/1/16		
"	17/1/16		
"	18/1/16		
"	19/1/16		
"	20/1/16		
F. pulvector	21/1/16	Battalion relieved 7th F/ rector. Batt: on right 8TH Suffolks. " " left. 2ND KOYLI.	
"	22/1/16	Enemy artillery active. Casualties. Wounded - 1 officer Killed 1 man 2 men	officer died evening 22/1/16
"	23/1/16	Day very quiet.	
"	24/1/16	" " "	
"	25/1/16	Our artillery bombarded the MOUND, with good results. 1 man wounded (peep in field)	

11TH BORDER REGT.
WAR DIARY
or
INTELLIGENCE SUMMARY.
(Erase heading not required.)

Army Form C. 2118.

Hour, Date, Place		Summary of Events and Information	Remarks and references to Appendices
F.I. Sector.	26/1/16.	Day quiet	
"	27/1/16	Our artillery bombarded new gun emplacement.	
"	28/1/16	17TH H.L.I relieved 11TH BORDER REST in F.I sector or 11TH BORDER REST went back to bivvies or AVELUY. Casualty 1 man killed.	
AVELUY	29/1/16	R.E. fatigues. at 6.55 PM 8 shells fell in AVELUY.	
AVELUY	30/1/16.	R.E. fatigues	
"	31/1/16	R.E. fatigues	

97th Brigade.

32nd Division

11th BATTALION

THE BORDER REGIMENT

FEBRUARY 1 9 1 6

32

11th Border Regt.
Vol: 3

ORIGINAL

11TH Border Regt

WAR DIARY
or
INTELLIGENCE SUMMARY
(Erase heading not required.)

Army Form C. 2118

Instructions regarding War Diaries and Intelligence Summaries are contained in F.S. Regs., Part II. and the Staff Manual respectively. Title Pages will be prepared in manuscript.

Place	Date	Hour	Summary of Events and Information	Remarks and references to Appendices
AVELUY	1/2/16		Batt in reserve. R.E. Fatigues.	
"	2/2/16		" " " " "	
"	3/2/16		" " " " "	
"	4/2/16		Relief of 17th H.L.I. postponed owing to a bombardment by our artillery.	
" Sector	5/2/16		11TH Border Regt relieved 17TH H.L.I. Draft of 29 O.R. received 5/2/16.	
			Batt on right :— 8TH SUFFOLKS.	
			Batt on left :— 2ND K.O.Y.L.I.	
			Casualties :— 2 wounded.	
"	6/2/16		Front very quiet.	
			Casualty. wounded 1. Shee shock 1.	
"	7/2/16		Front very quiet.	
"	8/2/16		" " "	
			~~Casualties. wounded~~	
"	9/2/16		Heavy bombardment of half of F1, and F2 subsectors.	6TH NORFOLKS relieved 8TH SUFFOLKS
			Casualties. killed 1. wounded 1. ~~Shell shock~~ 0	

11TH Border Regt.
WAR DIARY
INTELLIGENCE SUMMARY

Army Form C. 2118

Place	Date	Hour	Summary of Events and Information	Remarks and references to Appendices
1 Section	10/2/16		Front fairly quiet. Casualties:- Killed 1. Wounded 1. Shell shock 2.	
ALBERT	11/2/16		Front fairly quiet. 17TH HLI relieved 11TH Border Regt in F1 Sector. 11TH Border Regt relieved 10 inniskts in ALBERT. Casualties:- 1 Killed (NCO). Working party for R.E.	
"	12/2/16		"	
"	13/2/16		"	
"	14/2/16		"	
"	15/2/16		"	
"	16/2/16		"	
HENENCOURT	17/2/16		2ND INNISKILLING FUSILIERS relieved 11TH BORDER REGT in ALBERT. Border Regt relieved in turn in Henencourt Wood. 96TH Bge relieved 97TH Bge	
"	18/2/16		⎫	
"	19/2/16		⎬ Fatigues.	
"	20/2/16		⎭	
"	21/2/16			
"	22/2/16		Batt took on duty of readiness to move into reserve, at 6 PM 22 ND	

11TH Border Regt.

WAR DIARY
or
INTELLIGENCE SUMMARY.
(Erase heading not required.)

Army Form C. 2118.

Instructions regarding War Diaries and Intelligence
Summaries are contained in F.S. Regs., Part II
and the Staff Manual respectively. Title pages
will be prepared in manuscript.

Hour, Date, Place		Summary of Events and Information	Remarks and references to Appendices
HENENCOURT	23/2/16	Batt on duty.	
MILLENCOURT	24/2/16	11TH BORDER REST and 11TH HLI relieved each other	
"	25/2/16	11TH BORDER REST billets in MILLENCOURT	
"	27/2/16	Batt on Duty	
"	28/2/16	} Fatigues.	
"	29/2/16		

CW Margerison Lt: for Lt-Col:
Comdg: 11TH Border Regt.

11th Baden Vol 4

P. Avery

H.P.
5 sheet

11TH Border Regt.

WAR DIARY
or
INTELLIGENCE SUMMARY.
(Erase heading not required.)

Army Form C. 2118.

Instructions regarding War Diaries and Intelligence Summaries are contained in F.S. Regs., Part II and the Staff Manual respectively. Title pages will be prepared in manuscript.

Hour, Date, Place		Summary of Events and Information	Remarks and references to Appendices
1/3/16	HEVENCOURT	Billets.	
2/3/16	E I Sector	Battalion took over E I Sector from the 15TH H.L.I. The 97TH Bgd. taking over from the 14TH Bgd.	
3/3/16	"	⎫	
4/3/16	"	⎪ Front very quiet owing to bad weather.	
5/3/16	"	⎬ Snow, frost, and thaw alternating. Trenches falling in and very wet.	
6/3/16	"	⎪	
7/3/16	"	⎭ Trenches improving. Enemy shells in support line. Blown in burying 3 men. 1 severe shock. 2 killed. (since killed) In evening, 1 NCO wounded by piece of an H.E. shell.	
8/3/16	"	Front quiet.	
9/3/16	"	Enemy artillery sheeled working party, killing 2Lt Robinson, 1 NCO, and wounding 1 man. 2/1 man wounded by rifle grenade.	

11TH Border Regt.
WAR DIARY
or
INTELLIGENCE SUMMARY.
(Erase heading not required.)

Army Form C. 2118.

Hour, Date, Place		Summary of Events and Information	Remarks and references to Appendices
10/3/16	E I Sector	11TH Border Regt relieved by 17TH H.L.I. 11TH Border Regt billeted in ALBERT, less 1 platoon garrison of TARA REDOUBT.	
11/3/16	ALBERT	Working parties for R.E. etc. 1 other rank accidentally wounded	
12/3/16	"	Working parties for R.E. etc.	
13/3/16	"	" Draft, 1 officer, 30 other ranks.	(2/Lt Bourne)
14/3/16	"	" 2 Other ranks wounded.	
15/3/16	"	"	
16/3/16	"	"	
17/3/16	E I Sector	11TH Border Regt relieved 17TH H.L.I. in E I Sector 1 other rank wounded. Front very quiet.	
18/3/16	"	"	
19/3/16	"	" Been commenced.	
20/3/16	"	"	
21/3/16	"	" 2 Other ranks slightly wounded (shrapnel.) 2 Other ranks killed	
22/3/16	"	" 3 other ranks wounded } Rifle Grenade.	

WAR DIARY
or
INTELLIGENCE SUMMARY.
(Erase heading not required.)

Army Form C. 2118.

Instructions regarding War Diaries and Intelligence Summaries are contained in F.S. Regs., Part II and the Staff Manual respectively. Title pages will be prepared in manuscript.

Hour, Date, Place		Summary of Events and Information	Remarks and references to Appendices
23/3/16	DERNANCOURT	The 17TH HLI relieved the 11TH Border Regt. Border Regt filled in DERNANCOURT. 1 Coy left as garrison of Becourt Wood Defences. Rest billets.	
24/3/16	"	" "	
25/3/16	"	" "	
26/3/16	"	" "	
27/3/16	"	" "	
28/3/16	"	" "	
29/3/16	E I Sector	11TH Border Regt relieved 17TH HLI in E I Sector.	
30/3/16	"	Draft:- 2 officers. 22 O.R. Davidson's and MonAlone.	
31/3/16	"	Sector very quiet.	

C.W.Mogerison Lt.

97th Brigade.
32nd Division.

11th BATTALION

THE BORDER REGIMENT

APRIL 1916

11th Border Regt.

WAR DIARY
or
INTELLIGENCE SUMMARY

Army Form C. 2118.

11 Border 2g
vol 5

(Erase heading not required.)

Hour, Date, Place.		Summary of Events and Information	Remarks and references to Appendices
1/4/16.	E I Sector	Front very quiet. Draft of 20 men arrived on anger of 3D/3/16.	
2/4/16	"	" " Raid on German salient at x20D 7025 postponed owing to brightness of night.	
3/4/16.	"	" " Casualty :- 1 other rank. Bruised	
4/4/16.	Senlis	11TH Border Regt relieved by 10TH Y and L. Regt. Returned to Billets in Senlis	
5/4/16	"	Resting and cleaning up.	
6/4/16.	"	Started Coy. training & musketry, etc.	
7/4/16.	"	Coy. training, etc.	
8/4/16.	"	" Draft of 20 other ranks received.	
9/4/16.	"	"	
10/4/16	"	} Training	
11/4/16	"		
12/4/16	AVELUY	Batt. moved into support at AVELUY	
13/4/16	"	Working Parties.	
14/4/16	"	" A. Coy Proceeded to isolation camp at Senlis (measles).	
15/4/16	"	" 2nr Taylor accidentally killed.	
16/4/16.	"	"	

11th Batt Border Regt
WAR DIARY
or
INTELLIGENCE SUMMARY

Army Form C. 2118

(Erase heading not required.)

Instructions regarding War Diaries and Intelligence Summaries are contained in F. S. Regs., Part II. and the Staff Manual respectively. Title Pages will be prepared in manuscript.

Place	Date	Hour	Summary of Events and Information	Remarks and references to Appendices
Contay Wood	17/4/16		Batt went to isolation camp in CONTAY Wood.	
"	18/4/16		Batt Training. Small working parties.	
"	19/4/16		" " " "	
"	20/4/16		" " " "	
"	21/4/16		" " " "	Draft of 21 other ranks arrived.
"	22/4/16		" " " "	
"	23/4/16		" " " "	
"	24/4/16		" " " "	Draft of 2 officers 2Lt Green D Coy. 2Lt Mackrell C Coy.
"	25/4/16		⎫	
"	26/4/16		⎪	
"	27/4/16		⎬ Divisional & Bgd manoeuvres. Small daily working parties.	
"	28/4/16		⎪ Batt Training.	
"	29/4/16		⎪	
"	30/4/16		⎭	

C. Shaw-Gerson Lt.
11 Tt Batt Border Regt.

11 Border

11 TH Batt, Border Regt.

WAR DIARY
or
INTELLIGENCE SUMMARY.

XXXII Vol 6

Army Form C. 2118.

(Erase heading not required.)

C.P.
3rd set

Hour, Date, Place		Summary of Events and Information	Remarks and references to Appendices
CONTAY WOOD	1/5/16	Divisional & Regt manoeuvres. Batt Training. Smaller daily working parties.	
"	2/5/16		
"	3/5/16		
"	4/5/16		
"	5/5/16		Draft of 21 other ranks.
"	6/5/16	Divisional & Regt manoeuvres. Batt Training. Small daily working parties.	
"	7/5/16		
"	8/5/16		
"	9/5/16		Draft of 50 other ranks.
"	10/5/16		2Lt Bourne, C Coy, left the Batt and returned to England.
"	11/5/16		
"	12/5/16		
"	13/5/16		Batt out of isolation.
"	14/5/16	Batt Training	

Instructions regarding War Diaries and Intelligence Summaries are contained in F. S. Regs., Part II and the Staff Manual respectively. Title pages will be prepared in manuscript.

(73989) W4141—463. 400,000. 9/14. H.&J.Ltd. Forms/C. 2118/10.

11TH Border Regt.

WAR DIARY
or
INTELLIGENCE SUMMARY.

(Erase heading not required.)

Army Form C. 2118.

Hour, Date, Place	Summary of Events and Information	Remarks and references to Appendices
CONTAY WOOD 15/5/16.	Battalion training. Lts. E. Spring-Rice and C.W. Fowke reported their arrival.	
" 16/5/16	" "	
" 17/5/16.	Battalion moved from Contay to Bouzincourt.	
AUTHUILLE SECTOR 18/5/16	Battalion took over the Authuille Sector from the 19th Lancashire Fusiliers.	
	Party under Lt. Barnes remained in billets at Bouzincourt.	
AUTHUILLE " 19/5/16.	Artillery active on the night, otherwise quiet. Two Ors. O.R. wounded.	1. O.R. killed
" 20/5/16	" " " a few TMs on the right	
" "	Casualties 1 O.R. killed 2 O.R. wounded.	
" 21/5/16.	Battalion relieved by D Coy. initiated a chappel Front quiet	
CRUCIFIX CORNER 22/5/16	Battalion relieved by 17TH H.L.I. and billeted at CRUCIFIX CORNER'S. Coy. D Coy. billeted out in AVELUY.	
" 23/5/16.	Working parties supplied to work in AUTHUILLE SECTOR. Two O.R. wounded.	

Army Form C. 2118.

WAR DIARY
or
INTELLIGENCE SUMMARY
(Erase heading not required.)

Place	Date	Hour	Summary of Events and Information	Remarks and references to Appendices
BUCQUOY CORNER AUTHUILLE SECTOR	24/5/16		Supplied working parties in AUTHUILLE SECTOR. 2Lt T.C.R. MURPHY reported his arrival.	
"	25/5/16		" " " "	
AUTHUILLE SECTOR	26/5/16		Batt: relieved the 17TH H.L.I. in Authuille Sector. 2Lt G. Spring-Rice killed.	
"	27/5/16		Fairly quiet. Slight amount of T.M. activity.	
"	28/5/16		T.M. and artillery activity. 2Lt Rowan reported arrival.	
"	29/5/16		T.M. and artillery activity. 2Lt A.G. Smook, T.R.S. Rowan, A.J. Allan reported arrived. 7 O.R. wounded.	
BOIZINCOURT	30/5/16		Fairly quiet. 96TH Bge relieved 97TH Bge. 1 O R Killed. 11TH Borders relieved by 15TH L.F. 4 O R wounded. Left half Batt billeted in BOIZINCOURT Right " " bivouac " AVELUY WOOD.	
"	31/5/16		Working parties.	

C. Sharpsmann Lt.

97th Brigade.
32nd Division.

1/11th BATTALION

THE BORDER REGIMENT

JUNE 1916

11th Border Regt.
XXXII
Vol 7
11. Borders

WAR DIARY or INTELLIGENCE SUMMARY

Army Form C.2118.

Place	Date	Hour	Summary of Events and Information	Remarks and references to Appendices
BUZINCOURT.	1/6/16		Batt in Divisional Reserve. Working parties for R.E etc	
"	2/6/16		" " " " 226 W.S. Paton	
"	3/6/16		" " " " G. Beck	
"	4/6/16		" " " " Taken on strength of Batt.	
"	5/6/16		" " " "	
SENLIS	6/6/16		Party under Lt Barnes raided German trenches opposite R.31.1 Zero time 11 P.M. Casualties:— Lt Barnes and 5 O.R. Killed. 27 O.R. Wounded. 1 O.R. Wounded and Missing. 11 German prisoners captured. Battalion moved to billets in Senlis.	
"	7/6/16			
"	8/6/16		Divisional exercise on evening of 8th Battalion bivouacked the night 7th — 8th in BAVELINCOURT WOOD.	

1st Border Regt.
WAR DIARY

Army Form C. 2118

Instructions regarding War Diaries and Intelligence Summaries are contained in F.S. Regs., Part II. and the Staff Manual respectively. Title Pages will be prepared in manuscript.

(Erase heading not required.)

Place	Date	Hour	Summary of Events and Information	Remarks and references to Appendices
Senlis	9/6/16		Batt. Training.	
"	10/6/16		" "	
"	11/6/16		" "	
CONTAY	12/6/16		Divisional Ecercise. Battalion returns to billets in Contay.	
"	13/6/16		Bn Training.	
"	14/6/16		Divisional Exercise.	
"	15/6/16		Batt Training.	
"	16/6/16		" "	
"	17/6/16		" "	
"	18/6/16		" "	
"	19/6/16.		Bgn. Exercise.	
"	20/6/16.			Draft:- 5 other ranks. 1 O.R. wounded (unspecified)
"	21/6/16.		Divisional Exercise.	
"	22/6/16		The Batt moved to billets at BOUZINCOURT, arriving 12.20 AM 23/6/16.

11th Border Regt.

WAR DIARY
INTELLIGENCE SUMMARY

Army Form C. 2118.

Place	Date	Hour	Summary of Events and Information	Remarks and references to Appendices
AUTHUILE SECTOR	23/6/16		Batt. left Bouzincourt for the trenches, taking over from the 2ND MANCHESTER Regt at 12.30 AM 24/6/16.	
"	24/6/16		Our 18 Pounders commenced to cut the enemy wire at 5.30 AM and continued during the day. Enemy retaliation practically Nil. Gas raid on night 24-25 did not come off owing to unfavourable wind.	Casualties: 1 O.R. wounded, 2 O.R. shell shock
"	25/6/16		Our gun bombarded the German lines continuously. German retaliation very heavy during the afternoon.	
"	26/6/16		Continuous bombardment by both sides. We let off gas at 2.30 P.M. with apparent success. The 2ND KOYLI commenced to relieve us at 9.30 P.M.	2 OR killed, 30 OR wounded, 9 OR shell shock
CRUCIFIX CORNER	27/6/16		Relief complete at 12.40 AM 27th. Bombardment continued. B.II wiring S.A.A., grenades, etc.	

11th Border Regt
WAR DIARY
or
INTELLIGENCE SUMMARY
(Erase heading not required.)

Army Form C. 2118.

Place	Date	Hour	Summary of Events and Information	Remarks and references to Appendices
CRUCIFIX CORNER	28/6/16		Zero time postponed for 48 hours. Our artillery bombardment less intense.	
"	29/6/16		" " German retaliation slight.	
"	30/6/16		Batt. moved up to assembly trenches at 10 PM.	

A Wargnier Lt

97th Inf.Bde.
32nd Div.

WAR DIARY

11th BATTN. THE BORDER REGIMENT.

J U L Y

1 9 1 6

11th Border Regt.

WAR DIARY
or
INTELLIGENCE SUMMARY

(Erase heading not required.)

Army Form C. 2118

Place	Date	Hour	Summary of Events and Information	Remarks and references to Appendices
AUTHUILLE WOOD	1/7/16		Jest time 7.30am Battalion advanced from recently dug assembly trenches at 8am. and came under very heavy Machine Gun fire suffering 500 casualties. The following officers were killed - Lt Col Machulin CMG DSO, Capt. R. Smith, Capt A.E. Corbett Capt E. Actum, 2/Lt A.E. Mackense, 2/Lt J.C. Ruston, 2/Lt G. Cox, 2/Lt G.P. Dunstan, 2/Lt H.S. Palin, Lt. F.A. Rutt. Officers wounded - Major P.G.W. Diggle, Col. B.C. Harrison, Capt. C.P. Moore, Lieut W.A. Hobson, Lt C.H. Walker, Lt C.W. Thompson, Lt J.H. Stephenson, Lt. M. Golden, Lt. White Wilson, 2Lt J.R.S. Brown, 2LT J.W. Moore, 2Lt W Green, 2LT S Black, 2Lt F.M. Ranson, 2LT L. Meshell. Battalion assists in burying the dead and from fatigue for	
Authu..	2/7/16			
dU..	3/7/16		Carrying up glencade from Authuille Battalion withdrawn to Ennuich Aug. not	
Ennuift	4/7/16		Battalion found fatigue for returning and carrying up bombs to front line	

11th Bon la Regt.

WAR DIARY
or
INTELLIGENCE SUMMARY.
(Erase heading not required.)

Army Form C. 2118.

Hour, Date, Place	Summary of Events and Information	Remarks and references to Appendices
CRUCIFIX CORNER 4/7/16	Tonight the 4th-5th Battalion attached to 2nd Royal and marched to CONTAY WOOD.	
CONTAY WOOD 5/7/16 6/7/16 7/7/16	Reorganising into two Coys in CONTAY WOOD. Battalion strength 11 Officers & 480 O.R.	
SENLIS 8/7/16	Battalion marched to SENLIS and took over billets. Capt. Palmer 2nd K.O.Y.L.I. took over Command from Lt. Col. 2/Lts. Brown and King 17th H.L.I. attached.	
F1 SUB SECTOR 9/7/16	Battalion paraded at 8.0pm and marched to Trenches, taking over part of F1 Sub Sector one coy in front line, and one in Reserve.	
do 10/7/16 11/7/16	Battalion remained in line.	

11th Border Regt.

WAR DIARY
or
INTELLIGENCE SUMMARY
(Erase heading not required.)

Army Form C. 2118.

Place	Date	Hour	Summary of Events and Information	Remarks and references to Appendices
CRUCIFIX CORNER	10/7/16		Battalion withdrawn to Crucifix Cnr — Lt Kirkwood R.A.M.C. relieved by Lt Webster R.A.M.C.	
do	12/7/16 14/7/16 15/7/16		Battalion from fatigue front line — Major Chamber Engineer 10th B40 Rearse took over command from Capt Palmer 2 R.O.Y.L. on the 14/7/16. Notification Major Gratton D.S.O. took over command from Major Clarke Lyons & was appointed 2nd in Command on the 14/7/16	
BERTRENCOURT	16/7/16		Battalion withdrawn to Bertrencourt and billeted in huts	
	16/7/16		Battalion marched to AMPLIERS, via ACHEUX and SARTON and took over luck Divisional Command (General Clynch's address) Brigade conferences then on these movements — Battalion paraded at 2.55 pm and marched to Sus-St-Leger, via HALLOY - LUCHEUX - and took one nights Battalion arrived resting in Sur. St. Leger	
SUS ST LEGER	17/7/16			?
	18/7/16		— marches to NEUVILLE-AU-CORNET via BEAUDICOURT ÉTRÉE-WAMIN - HOUVIN-HOUVIGNEUL.	

11th Rifles Regt.

WAR DIARY or INTELLIGENCE SUMMARY

Army Form C. 2118.

Place	Date	Hour	Summary of Events and Information	Remarks and references to Appendices
	20/7/16.		Battalion marched to CONTEVILLE, via OSTREVILLE - BRYAS, and for on billets. The following Officers reported their arrival and are taken on the strength of the Battalion. Lt. D.W. Bury, Lt. Col. McLennan, 2/Lt. J.H. Armour, 2/Lt. R.R. Spence, 2/Lt. G/G. Birkins, 2/Lt. F. Story, 2/Lt. Col. Wilson, 2/Lt. R.S. Orr.	
	21/7/16.		Battalion marched to ALLOUAGNE, via PARNES - FLORINGHEM - AUCHEL - LOZINGHEM and for in billets.	
LLOUAGNE	22/7/16.		Battalion remained in billets - baths and clean clothing issued. The undermentioned Officers reported their arrival and were taken on the strength of the Battalion. Major F. Luke Guise, Capt M.G. Nelson, Capt C.D. Dove, 2/Lt Lt. John Patten, 2/Lt W.L. Allcroft, 2/Lt W.J. L. Stone, 2/Lt W.R. Gillespie.	
LLOUAGNE	23/7/16.		Church Parade at 11.0 a.m. The Rev. Crone presided.	
"	24/7/16.		The Battalion paraded in the morning for Kit and in the afternoon for Kit inspection.	

11th Border Regt

WAR DIARY or INTELLIGENCE SUMMARY

Army Form C. 2118.

Place	Date	Hour	Summary of Events and Information	Remarks and references to Appendices
LOUAGNE	25/7/16		Battalion paraded for drill in the morning under Company arrangements, and for Gas Helmet and Gun Calibre inspection in the afternoon.	
	26/7/16		The Battalion marched to BETHUNE via PONT DE REVEILLON – CHOCQUES and took on billets.	
BETHUNE	27/7/16		Battalion paraded for physical drill and rifle exercises in the morning and the afternoon an extra Fatiguing Party equipment etc.	
	28/7/16		The Battalion marched to point J.6.a.7.7 for inspection by General Thwaites, Commanding 1st Army. The 14th & 97th Brigades were on parade in marching order. The Battalion was congratulated by the Army Commander on its smart appearance and steadiness on parade, and marched back to Billets in BETHUNE.	
	29/7/16		The Battalion was attached to the 8th Division MINES and HOHENZOLLERN being billeted whilst in NOYELLES.	
NOYELLES	30/7/16		Battalion furnishing parties for MAXPIM Stem Gear etc. of	
"	31/7/16		Carrying parties for mining. Carrying parties for mining.	

E.C. Ashford Major
Comdg. 11th Border Regt.

97th Brigade.
32nd Division.

11th BATTALION

THE BORDER REGIMENT

AUGUST 1 9 1 6

CONFIDENTIAL.

War Diary
of
11th Border Regiment

from 1st August 1916 to 31st August 1916
(Volume 9)

Army Form C. 2118.

WAR DIARY
or
INTELLIGENCE SUMMARY

(Erase heading not required.)

Instructions regarding War Diaries and Intelligence Summaries are contained in F. S. Regs., Part II. and the Staff Manual respectively. Title Pages will be prepared in manuscript.

Place	Date	Hour	Summary of Events and Information	Remarks and references to Appendices

2449 Wt. W14957/M90 750,000 1/16 J.B.C. & A. Forms/C.2118/12.

WAR DIARY
or
INTELLIGENCE SUMMARY

(Erase heading not required.)

Army Form C. 2118.

Place	Date	Hour	Summary of Events and Information	Remarks and references to Appendices
NOYELLE	1/8/16	10 P.M.	B Officers and 2 I.S.O.R. during mining fatigues at HOHENZOLLERN REDOUBT & the HAIRPIN MINES. D & C sight of SQ.O.R. joined the Battalion during the morning. JM	
"	2/8/16	10 P.M.	Parties still doing mining fatigues. JM	
"	3/8/16	10 P.M.	All working parties were relieved by the 21st Infantry Brigade at 12.30 P.M. from HOHENZOLLERN REDOUBT & HAIRPIN MINES. They proceeded to NOYELLE foret at 1.30 P.M. A party of 4 officers and 110 O.R. proceeded to ANNEQUIN to form working parties for the 2nd MANCHESTERS. JM	
"	4/8/16	10 P.M.	During morning there was kit inspection by Company Commanders JM	
CAMBRIN SECTOR	5/8/16	10 P.M.	Battalion left NOYELLE for support trenches in the CAMBRIN SECTOR arriving at 5.15 P.M. Battalion relieved the 1st SHERWOOD FORESTERS. Battalion strength in trenches 20 officers (including M.O.) and 280 O.R. Battalion H.Q. MAISON ROUGE. During afternoon hostile observation balloons were up. They were taken down at 6 P.M. The Commanding Officer visited SIMS KEEP & ARTHURS KEEP and found all in order. JM	
"	6/8/16	10 P.M.	Day spent in improving trenches etc. Artillery on both sides was quiet, but aeroplanes were continually over the german lines observing. Hostile aeroplanes made several attempts to cross our lines but were quickly driven back by our artillery. The Commanding Officer visited SIMS KEEP & ARTHURS KEEP at 10 P.M. and found both in good order. Machine guns in both sides were very active. Ennuis Trench Mortars were active along our lines doing no material damage. Our T.M.s replied effectively. JM	
"	7/8/16	10 P.M.	The Corps Commander G.S.O.1 & C.R.E. of 32nd Division visited Battalion H.Q. during morning. At 2 P.M. the Commanding Officer visited the right of the sub sector (portion of our Battalion takeover.) In HIGH ST the enemy were very active with Trench Mortars. There was no retaliation from our guns. At 9 P.M. the engineers exploded a mine in the left sub sector. There was considerable artillery activity for about an hour. JM	
"	8/8/16	10 P.M.	4 Officers commanding the Battalions in the 96th Infantry Brigade visited Battalion H.Q. They called for the purpose of getting information of the trenches which they are to take over. JM	

WAR DIARY or INTELLIGENCE SUMMARY

Army Form C. 2118.

(Erase heading not required.)

Instructions regarding War Diaries and Intelligence Summaries are contained in F. S. Regs., Part II. and the Staff Manual respectively. Title Pages will be prepared in manuscript.

Place	Date	Hour	Summary of Events and Information	Remarks and references to Appendices
CAMBRIN SECTOR (SENT TO)	9/8/16	10 P.M.	Brigadier-General Yatman of the 96th Infantry Brigade visited Battalion HQ.	
FRONT LINE TRS. (RAILWAY KEEP) Battn. H.Q.	10/8/16	10 P.M.	Battalion took over the front line trenches with the right of the sub-sector (Cambrin Sector) Battalion relieved the 1/9th H.L.I. at 2 P.M. The 1/6th K.O.Y.L.S. relieved our Battalion in support line. At 9 P.M. the relief was carried out successfully without any casualties. The 1/6th K.O.Y.L.S relieved our Battalion in support line. At 9 P.M. the relief was carried out successfully without any casualties. The Commanding Officer at 1 A.M. During the day T.M's were active. Both Major Chantaleyne visited the trenches. At 9 P.M. Major Chantaleyne visited the trenches. Hostile and our own A.M.G. were heard by a T.M. gun. A gun was damaged.	
"	11/8/16	10 P.M.	Day was comparatively quiet. A few Hostile TM's were sent over during the day doing no material damage, our TM's replied with good success. During the night of the 10th portions of the 1/9th H.L.I. were sent out to act as working parties for cleaning trenches etc. The Commanding Officer visited the trenches at 9 P.M. and Major Chantaleyne at 1 A.M.	
"	12/8/16	10 P.M.	Early this morning N.C.O & 1 O.R. (M.G.) were hit by an explosive bullet. At 8 A.M. Germans were killed. Hostile artillery was very quiet during morning. At 4·10 P.M. our artillery bombarded for 15 m. in the German lines. At 8 P.M. the Germans started a bombardment which lasted about an hour, our artillery replied very effectively causing the enemy to cease their fire. There was 3 O.R. wounded in the bombardment. The Commanding Officer visited the trenches at 9·30 P.M.	
"	13/8/16	10 P.M.	Day was quiet. At 5 P.M. the enemy exploded a mine near the HOHENZOLLERN REDOUBT clouds of dust were formed. At 4·30 a.m. a bombing group in No Mans Land were heard moving, 2 of our bombers (Grans) & Hesseland our forms. At 4·30 a.m. a bomb amongst a man who at once replied during the enemy away. At 9·30 P.M. the Officer Commanding the K.O.Y.L.S visited Battalion H.Q.	

WAR DIARY
or
INTELLIGENCE SUMMARY

(Erase heading not required.)

Army Form C. 2118.

Place	Date	Hour	Summary of Events and Information	Remarks and references to Appendices
ANNEQUIN (RESERVE)	14/8/16	10 P.M.	At 2 P.M. the Battalion was relieved by the 19th H.L.I. The relief was carried out successfully & was completed by 6 P.M. The Battalion returned to ANNEQUIN in billets. 3 p O.R. joined the Battalion at 5.30 P.M. JMcR	
,,	15/8/16	10 P.M.	14 O.R. joined the Battalion at 4 P.M. Half of the Battalion had baths and clean underclothes were issued. The Commanding Officer delivered a lecture on intelligence at 5.30 P.M. JMcR	
,,	16/8/16	10 P.M.	Brigadier General Jardine visited Battalion H.Q. at 12.30 P.M. and selected a place for Advanced Brigade H.Q. Half the Battalion had baths and clean clothes were issued. JMcR	
CAMBRIN SECTOR (LEFT LINE TRS) RAILWAY KEEP (BATT N H.Q.)	17/8/16	10 P.M.	Battalion left ANNEQUIN for front line trenches in the CAMBRIN SECTOR and relieved 14th H.L.I. in the right of the sub-sector at 2 A.M. Relief completed by 4.15 A.M. Enemy comparatively quiet. JMcR	
,,	18/8/16	10 P.M.	G.S.O.3 visited Battn H.Q. in morning. Commanding Officer visited front line trenches in the right sub-sector at 8.45 P.M. returning at 11.30 P.M. During morning it was very quiet along the whole sector. T.M's were active in afternoon (Hostile) Evening quiet. JMcR	
,,	19/8/16	10 P.M.	Day comparatively quiet. An R.E. & Artillery officer visited Battn H.Q. during morning. The Commanding Officer visited right sub-sector (trenches) at 9.15 A.M. returning 10.15 A.M. Weather and trenches in good condition. JMcR	

WAR DIARY or INTELLIGENCE SUMMARY

Army Form C. 2118.

Place	Date	Hour	Summary of Events and Information	Remarks and references to Appendices
,,	20/8/16	10 P.M.	Day comparatively quiet but for a few T.M. fire from both sides also Rifle grenades, etc. JM	
BETHUNE	21/8/16	10 P.M.	Battalion relieved in trenches by 15th Lancashire Fusiliers, Relief commenced 1:30 P.M. completed at 4:30 P.M. Battn took over Billets in BETHUNE. JM	
,,	22/8/16	10 P.M.	Battn found the following guards (4) R.T.O. inspection by Coy Commanders. 2nd Lt. Heroft returned to Battn from Lewis Gun Course JM	
PHILOSOPHE	23/8/16	10 P.M.	Commanding Officer & Company Commanders left BETHUNE at 10AM to inspect trenches in HULLUCH SECTOR. Battalion left BETHUNE at 12 Noon to take over Billets at PHILOSOPHE from Royal Dublin Fusiliers. Men Baths. 5 Officers returned from Divisional School trench strength 305 OR. 15 Officers JM	
(SUPPORT TR) HULLUCH SECTOR	24/8/16	10 P.M.	Battalion left PHILOSOPHE at 11AM for Support trenches in HULLUCH SECTOR relieving Royal Irish Rifles. Relief completed 11:30 P.M. Our aeroplanes very active during afternoon reversing our German lines. Trench strength 15 officers 305 OR. JM	
,,	25/8/16	10 P.M.	At 11·40 P.M. on the 24th. similate a raid was carried out by the 25th Brigade on the left of the sector, but Artillery bombed for our front, Day was comparatively quiet. Brigadier General Jardine visited Battn H.Q. during morning. JM	

WAR DIARY
or
INTELLIGENCE SUMMARY
(Erase heading not required.)

Army Form C. 2118.

Place	Date	Hour	Summary of Events and Information	Remarks and references to Appendices
"	24/8/16	10 P.M.	Day very quiet. At 10.30 a.m. the Commanding Officer inspected 17th H.L.I. Battn H.Q. At 2 A.m. commanding officer visited front line trenches which will be taken over by the battalion on the 28th instant. Conference was held at Battn H.Q. by Brigadier General Jardine. JM	
"	27/8/16	10 P.M.	Day very quiet. At 10 A.M. a conference was held at Battn H.Q. by Brigadier General Jardine. Commanding Officers Commanding Battalions were present. JM	
FRONT LINE TRENCHES (HULLUCH SECTOR)	28/8/16	10 P.M.	At 12.30 a.m. battalion relieved the 17th H.L.I. in the front line trenches (left of HULLUCH SECTOR) Relief completed by 2.45 a.m. Day very quiet. Commanding Officer inspected the front line trenches during the night. JM	
"	29/8/16	10 P.M.	A bombardment of the enemies lines from (H.19.a.½.4) to (H.13a.5t.54) was carried out at 4.20 p.m. by our Field guns, 4.5 Hows. Medium & light T.M's & Rifle grenade batteries. It lasted for 30 mins. There was very little retaliation. The enemies trenches were badly damaged. From 4.30 p.m. to 10.30 p.m. it rained very heavily causing some damage to our trenches & dug outs. JM	

WAR DIARY
or
INTELLIGENCE SUMMARY

(Erase heading not required.)

Army Form C. 2118.

Place	Date	Hour	Summary of Events and Information	Remarks and references to Appendices
?	30/8/16	10 PM	Day comparatively quiet. Officers of 8th Brigade 3rd Division visited trenches before taking over the line from 32nd Division. yfh	
BETHUNE.	31/8/16	10 PM.	Battn was relieved at 2.30am by Royal Scots 3rd Division. Relief completed at 4 am. Battn proceeded to BETHUNE to rest billets. yfh	

J Monteith Lt MA

AB Maitland Lt Col
Comdg 11th Border Regt

97th Brigade.

32nd Division.

11th BATTALION

THE BORDER REGIMENT

SEPTEMBER 1 9 1 6

Confidential.

War Diary

of

11th Border Regt.

from 1st September,1916 to 30th September,1916.

Volume 10.

Army Form C. 2118.

WAR DIARY
or
INTELLIGENCE SUMMARY

(Erase heading not required.)

M Barton R

Instructions regarding War Diaries and Intelligence Summaries are contained in F. S. Regs., Part II. and the Staff Manual respectively. Title Pages will be prepared in manuscript.

Place	Date	Hour	Summary of Events and Information	Remarks and references to Appendices
BETHUNE.	1/9/16	10 PM	Battalion in billets at BETHUNE. Companies were inspected by the Company Commanders. All men had a bath and clean clothes. At 5 p.m. there was a lecture for officers & N.C.O.s on bayonet fighting at the theatre.	
,,	2/9/16	10 PM	Battalion paraded at 8 a.m. and marched to the Champ de Tir for a days training. Batt returned to billets 4.30 p.m.	
,,	3/9/16	10 PM	Batt paraded at 9.45 a.m. and were taken by bus to the CAMBRIN SECTOR for work on the communication trenches. Batt returned to billets at 3.30 p.m.	
,,	4/9/16	10 PM	Companies at the disposal of the Company Commanders during the morning. Inspection & recreation in the afternoon. Commanding Officer martial Brigade H.Q. Shortly unveiled.	
,,	5/9/16	10 PM	Companies at the disposal of Company Commanders during morning. Commanding Officer & Intelligence Officer attended a lecture on air photos in the afternoon 5.30 p.m.	
,,	6/9/16	10 PM	Batt paraded 8.30 a.m. for route march and proceeded via VERQUIN, VAUDRICOURT, HOUCHIN, and HAILLICOURT, returning to billets at 12.15 p.m. Afternoon given up to recreation.	
,,	7/9/16	10 PM	Companies at the disposal of Company Commanders during morning. Most of afternoon taken up for recreation. Doctors medical inspection at 2.30 p.m.	

WAR DIARY
or
INTELLIGENCE SUMMARY

Army Form C. 2118.

1/5th Border R.

Place	Date	Hour	Summary of Events and Information	Remarks and references to Appendices
RESERVE BILLETS AT QUESNOY (CUINCHY SECTOR)	8/9/16	10P.M.	Battn. left BETHUNE for QUESNOY to take up Reserve position in the CUINCHY SECTOR. Relief commenced 1.30 A.M. & was completed by 2.15 A.M.	
"	9/9/16	10P.M.	Companies at the disposal of Company Commanders during morning. M.G. & I.O. visited Battn. H.Q. of the 17th H.L.I during morning. Company Commanders visited the front line trenches before taking over from 17th H.L.I. on the 12th instant.	
"	10/9/16	10.P.M.	Companies at the disposal of Company Commanders during morning. The Commanding Officer attended a conference of C.O.s held by Brigadier General Jardine at Lefont H.Q. in HARLEY STREET. At 4 P.M. a major general Kempt visited Bn. H.Q. m A voluntary service was held at B.H.Q., conducted by Captain Martin.	
"	11/9/16	10P.M.	Companies at the disposal of Company Commanders during morning. Afternoon given up to recreation. Commanding officer attended a conference of brigade officers.	
FRONT LINE TRs CUINCHY SECTOR	12/9/16	10P.M.	Battn. relieved the 17th H.L.I. in front line trenches. Relief commenced 12.45 P.M completed at 4.30 A.M.	
"	13/9/16	10P.M	Brigadier General Jardine conducted a tour round back line positions & machine gun positions with the officer commanding batts of the 97th Brigade. Day was comparatively quiet at few Hostile T.M.s fell near our front line & obstacle doing no damage. Hostile machine guns very active during evening.	

WAR DIARY or INTELLIGENCE SUMMARY

Army Form C. 2118.

11th Bn Border R.

Place	Date	Hour	Summary of Events and Information	Remarks and references to Appendices
,,	14/9/16	10 A.M.	Commanding officer visited front line trenches & Company HQ during morning	
,,	15/9/16	10 P.M.	Day confidently quiet. At 4 p.m. hostile aerial darts & a few minenwerfers & shrapnel in direction of Brickstacks & searching for Stokes gun positions	
RESERVE LINE (HARLEY STREET) (BILLETS)	16/9/16	10 P.M.	Day confidently quiet. At 9.45 p.m. a raid was carried out by a party from the Royal Scots Day quiet. Battn was relieved in front line trenches by 14th H.L.I. & retired to Reserve line (Billets) HARLEY STREET. Relief commenced 3 p.m. & was completed 5 p.m.	
,, ,,	17/9/16	10 P.M.	Battn found working parties for front line trenches & R.E.s	
,, ,,	18/9/16	10 P.M.	Battn found working parties for front line trenches & R.E.'s Colonel Wace G.S.O. called at B". H.Q. during morning. Adjutant and other officers of the 11th Brigade were conducted round Nos 2 & 3 tracks by Brigadier General Jardine in morning	
,, ,,	19/9/16	10 P.M.	Battn found working parties for front line trenches & R.E. General Bycroft visited Bn H.Q. at 4.45 p.m.	
FRONT LINE TRENCHES CLANCHY SECTOR	20/9/16	10 P.M.	Battn relieved the 14th H.L.I. in front line trenches. Relief commenced 3 p.m. completed 4.45 a.m. Germans bombarded our line & from 6.45 p.m. to 7.15 p.m. Emergency our trenches.	

WAR DIARY or INTELLIGENCE SUMMARY

Army Form C. 2118.

1/Bn Border R

Place	Date	Hour	Summary of Events and Information	Remarks and references to Appendices
,,	21/9/16	10 P.M.	Day comparatively quiet. Commanding Officer visited front line trenches during morning. At 9.15 A.M. our 9½" howitzers bombarded enemies trenches for 1 hour. Very little retaliation. Colonel Aggs visited Bn. H.Q. during evening.	
off ,,	22/9/16	10 P.M.	Day comparatively quiet. Commanding Officer visited front line trenches during morning.	
off ,,	23/9/16	10 P.M.	During morning & afternoon enemy fired a number of equal dates & a few T.M's in direction of Buckstack doing no material damage. Enemy artillery (77m.m) fired a number of rounds in direction of CUINCHY CHURCH at 4 p.m. bombarding effect noted front line trenches during afternoon. Brigadier General Fortine visited Bn. H.Q. at 11.45 a.m.	
LE QUESNOY (RESERVE) off	24/9/16	10 P.M.	Commanding Officer visited front line trenches at 9.30 a.m. Battn. was relieved by 19th L.I. in front the trenches & proceeded to LE QUESNOY to be in Reserve. Relief commenced 2 p.m. & was completed 4.30 p.m.	
,, off	25/9/16	10 P.M.	Battn. found working parties for front line trenches & R.E. Commanding Officer visited a demonstration by teams from battns of 96th Brigade of the various ways of getting over craters, during afternoon.	

Army Form C. 2118.

WAR DIARY
or
INTELLIGENCE SUMMARY

(Erase heading not required.)

Instructions regarding War Diaries and Intelligence Summaries are contained in F.S. Regs., Part II and the Staff Manual respectively. Title Pages will be prepared in manuscript.

Place	Date	Hour	Summary of Events and Information	Remarks and references to Appendices
ANNEZIN	26/9/16	10 P.M.	Battn was relieved by 16th December Fusiliers from LE QUESNOY and proceeded to take over billets at ANNEZIN. Relief commenced 2 p.m. & was completed 3.45 p.m.	
,,	27/9/16	10 P.M.	Companies at the disposal of Company Commanders. Examining kits etc & cleaning equipment.	
,,	28/9/16	10 P.M.	Battn found working parties for front line trenches in the CAMBRIN SECTOR, at 2.30 a.m. Bgde carried out a practice with No 2 Sqdn R.F.C. in signalling the 97th Brigade carried out a practice in signalling. 2 per Company proceeded to take up 11th Border Regt consisting of 1 officer & a position in SAILLY LA BOURSE line (BEUVRY) at 12 noon, all took part in the practice.	
,,	29/9/16	10 P.M.	Companies at the disposal of Company Commanders during morning. Commanding Officer M.O. & 1 officer & 2 N.C.O's per Company attended a course on Gas at BEUVRY) commencing 7.30 a.m. In afternoon Companies went for one hour route march.	
,,	30/9/16	10 P.M.	Battn had baths in BETHUNE during morning. Commanding Officer visited billets during morning.	

Signed [signature]
O.C. ,, "B" Bn., Border Regt

11th Border Regt

97th Brigade.
32nd Division.

11th BATTALION

THE BORDER REGIMENT

OCTOBER 1 9 1 6

Vol 11

11.P
Cohort

Confidential.
War Diary
of
11th Border Regiment,
from 1st October, 1916. to 31st October 1916.
(Volume 11).

WAR DIARY
INTELLIGENCE SUMMARY

Army Form C. 2118.

11 Roden R.

Place	Date	Hour	Summary of Events and Information	Remarks and references to Appendices
ANNEZIN	1/10/16	10 P.M.	Battn practical crossing craters during morning. Commanding Officer was a member of a general court martial.	
"	2/10/16	10 P.M.	Battn practical crossing craters during morning. Adjutant visited Bn. H.Q. in CAMBRIN SECTOR. Sector Battn is to take over. Commanding Officer witnessed battn crossing craters during morning. Very wet afternoon.	
"	3/10/16	10 P.M.	Battn found fatigues for R.E. during morning. No parades owing to wet weather. In afternoon Battn practical crossing craters. General Pycroft was present.	
CAMBRIN SECTOR FRONT LINE TKS	4/10/16	10 P.M.	Battn left ANNEZIN for front line trenches in CAMBRIN SECTOR, relieving 1st DORSET REGT. (14th Brigade). Relief commenced 11:30am and was completed 4:15 A.M. At 4:55 and 6:14 P.M. & 2 gas & combined shoot of Stokes guns, Rifle fire, D.M.G. fire was carried out by 8th Division lasting for 5 min (each shoot). Battn co-operated with rifle & M.G. fire. Enemy retaliated with a few minenwerfer & 6 cm. cms.	
"	5/10/16	10 P.M.	G.S.O.1 Colonel Weer visited Bn. H.Q. at 9:55 am. Commanding Officer & Colonel Weer visited front line trenches. At 8 pm a strafe on the enemies trenches (8 Division) was carried out lasting till 9:35am. Gas & smoke being sent over at intervals & short bombardment by our T.M's. M.G. & Rifle fire.	

WAR DIARY
or
INTELLIGENCE SUMMARY

(Erase heading not required.)

Army Form C. 2118.

11 Border R.

Place	Date	Hour	Summary of Events and Information	Remarks and references to Appendices
"	6/10/16	10 P.M.	Day comparatively quiet. Commanding Officer visited front line trenches during morning. At 11.45am a bombardment of the enemies trenches was carried out by our Stokes & 2" T.M.P. Enemies trenches damaged considerably. No retaliation.	
"	7/10/16	10 P.M.	Day very quiet. Major Moore (14th H.L.I.) visited Bn H.Q. at 3pm and went round front line trenches with the Commanding Officer. During morning Commanding Officer attended a conference conducted by Brigadier General [Gordine?].	
CAMBRIN SECTOR (SUPPORT LINE)	8/10/16	10 P.M.	During morning Brigadier General [Erskine?] & Commanding Officer visited front line trenches. At 3pm the Battalion was relieved from the Right Sub Sector by the 14th H.L.I. and proceeded to take up position in [Village de vie?].	
"	9/10/16	10 P.M.	Major Wallace F.S.10.³ visited Bn. H.Q. during afternoon. Battn found working parties for R.E. Battn in the line during the day.	
"	10/10/16	10 P.M.	Battn found working parties for R.E. Draft of 20 men arrived as reinforcements for the Battn.	SPW

WAR DIARY or INTELLIGENCE SUMMARY

(Erase heading not required.)

1/Border R.

Army Form C. 2118.

Place	Date	Hour	Summary of Events and Information	Remarks and references to Appendices
CAMBRIN SECTOR	11/10/16	10 p.m	Battn in Support line (VILLAGE LINE) Supplied R.E. parties. C.O. Col GIRDWOOD proceeded to England on leave. Major MOORE D.S.O. 2 i/c took over command of Battn. Reinforcements of 2/12 O.R. arrived for Battn.	S/Sd
"	12/10/16	"	C.O. and party of 1st E. YORKS arrived prior to taking over line from us.	S/Sd
"	13/10/16	"	Battn in Reserve line. Supplied R.E. parties. Verd with Battn of Brig Gen JARDINE	S/Sd
BETHUNE	14/10/16	"	Battn left trenches for BETHUNE having been relieved by 1st E. YORKS. Supplied R.E. parties.	S/Sd
LABEUVRERE	15/10/16	"	Battn left BETHUNE full marching order. Arrived LABEUVRERE and billetted there. Battn trained in afternoon under C.O.	S/Sd
MONCHY BRETON	16/10/16	"	Battn left LABEUVRERE full marching order. Arrived MONCHY BRETON 1 p.m. Remained there overnight	S/Sd
MONCHEAUX	17/10/16	"	Battn left MONCHY BRETON full marching order arriving MONCHEAUX at 3 p.m.	S/Sd
LONGUEVILLETE	18/10/16	"	Battn left MONCHEAUX full marching order and arrived LONGUEVILLETE at 3.15 p.m.	S/Sd

WAR DIARY
—or—
INTELLIGENCE SUMMARY
(Erase heading not required.)

Army Form C. 2118.

11 Border R.

Place	Date	Hour	Summary of Events and Information	Remarks and references to Appendices
LONGUEVILLETE	19/10/16	10 pm	Battn left LONGUEVILLETE for HERISSAT. Full marching order. Marched for two hours and returned to LONGUEVILLETE.	SP 16
"	20/10/16	"	Battn remained in billets. During day Battn paraded for general instruction & bombing, throughout morning.	SP 16
"	21/10/16	"	6 am all marching order and arrived Battn left LONGUEVILLETE. Parade for general training. HERISSAT 1.45 pm	SP 16
HERISSAT	22/10/16	"	Battn remained in HERISSAT. Battn parade in morning. Live firing throughout morning. Bombing & firearms. C.O. Lt. GIRDWOOD rejoined Batt. Re-inforcement of 6 men arrived.	SP 16
"	23/10/16	"	Battn left HERISSAT for BOUZINCOURT 11.45 am. arrived BOUZINCOURT 6.15 pm.	SP 16
BOUZINCOURT	24/10/16	"	Battn in BOUZINCOURT. General parade & instruction.	SP 16
"	25/10/16	"	" R.E. working parties.	SP 16
"	26/10/16	"	"	SP 16
"	27/10/16	"	"	SP 16
"	28/10/16	"	S.O.C. (Sir Haig) in company with D.C. Brigade & firing rifles, rifles & also Congratulated C.O. 11 Borders on the state of his Battn.	S

WAR DIARY
or
INTELLIGENCE SUMMARY

Army Form C. 2118.

1/Dorset R.

Place	Date	Hour	Summary of Events and Information	Remarks and references to Appendices
BOUZINCOURT	29/10/16	10 pm	Batt'n in BOUZINCOURT. General marches R.E. practice.	SPh
HERISSAT	30/10/16	10 pm	Batt'n left BOUZINCOURT. Full marching order, arrived at 11.30 am in HERISSAT.	SPh
LA VICOGNE	31/10/16	"	Batt'n left HERISSAT. Full marching order, arrived at LA VICOGNE.	SPh

R.L. Girdwood Lt Col
Comdg 1st Dorset Regt

97th Brigade.

32nd Division.

11th BATTALION

THE BORDER REGIMENT

NOVEMBER 1 9 1 6

CONFIDENTIAL.

War Diary
of
11th Border Regiment
from 1/11/16 to 30/11/16.
(Volume 12).

Army Form C. 2118

WAR DIARY
or
INTELLIGENCE SUMMARY

(Erase heading not required.)

Instructions regarding War Diaries and Intelligence Summaries are contained in F.S. Regs., Part II. and the Staff Manual respectively. Title Pages will be prepared in manuscript.

Place	Date	Hour	Summary of Events and Information	Remarks and references to Appendices

1875 Wt. W593/826 1,000,000 4/15 J.B.C. & A. A.D.S.S./Forms/C. 8.

Place	Date	Hour	Summary of Events and Information	Remarks and references to Appendices
LA VICOGNE	1/10/16	10 p.m.	General Parade of Junction for the Batt. under C.O.	S.S.6
"	2/10/16	"	Batt. took part in Brigade Field Day. At 2.25 p/m Batt. took up a position in artillery formation beyond a wood 2000 yds WEST of HERISSAT near TALMAS and HERISSAT road. Batt. at 2.30 p/m advanced in westerly direction on bearing approx; 300°M. Leading Coy A having through VAL DE MAISON at 3.23 p/m followed by B.C & D. Coy's Rear of Battn passed at 3.35 p/m no of formation. At 3.45 p/m Battn broke into extended order (A. Coy at 3.45, B. at 3.50 pm. C & D Coys at 3.52 p/m) making an advance of four waves at 100 yds interval on LA VICOGNE. Rear of Battn experienced difficulties at 4.10 p/m the two rear Coy's becoming mixed. Country rough reinforced with deep gullie about 2100 yds WEST of VAL DE MAISON 300°M bearing held up Coy's mixed slightly disorganised. Battn again advanced at 4.30 p/m hy[?]ll over rough ground and reached LA VICOGNE Rear of Battn had passed through 4.40 p/m. Position of Consolidation occupied at western side LA VICOGNE at 4.43 p/m & patrols pushed forward.	S.S.6 12 P grant

11th Border Regt
97 / 32

Army Form C. 2118.

1/4th Border Regt

WAR DIARY
or
INTELLIGENCE SUMMARY

(Erase heading not required.)

Instructions regarding War Diaries and Intelligence Summaries are contained in F. S. Regs., Part II. and the Staff Manual respectively. Title Pages will be prepared in manuscript.

Place	Date	Hour	Summary of Events and Information	Remarks and references to Appendices
VICOGNE	3/11/16	10 p.m	General parades of instruction under C.O.	S/o/b
"	4/11/16	"	" " " " "	S/o/b
"	5/11/16	"	" " " extended order drill etc	S/o/b
"	6/11/16	"	Battn took part in Brigade Field Day. Advanced from a position South VAL DE MAISON and marched towards BEAUVAL, trailing into artillery formation when necessary & finally operation South of BEHENCOURT having taken into extended order at FMC du ROCE.	S/o/b
"	7/11/16	"	General parades of instruction.	S/o/b
"	8/11/16	"	" " " "	S/o/b
"	9/11/16	"	Battn went for route march under C.O.	S/o/b
"	10/11/16	"	General parade.	S/o/b
"	11/11/16	"	Visit of Brigadier (JARDINE) to meet all officers of 94th Brigade. Bugler appears under C.O. for tactical scheme parade.	S/o/b
"	12/11/16	"	Church parade.	S/o/b

WAR DIARY or INTELLIGENCE SUMMARY

Army Form C. 2118.

11th Border Regt.

Place	Date	Hour	Summary of Events and Information	Remarks and references to Appendices
CONTAY	13/11/16	10 p.m.	Orders received to march. Batt'n left LA VICOGNE at 10 a.m. and arrived CONTAY 3 p.m.	S.Th.
BLACK HORSE BRIDGE.	14/11/16	"	Batt'n left CONTAY full marching order 1 p.m. and arrived BLACK HORSE BRIDGE 9 p.m. Trying march for Batt'n & little accommodation for men.	S.Th.
ENGLEBELMER	15/11/16	"	Orders received to dump packs etc. Then marched in Battle order and at 2 p.m. marched for ENGLEBELMER arriving 5 p.m.	S.Th.
"	16/11/16	"	Batt'n remained in ENGLEBELMER fitting out with bombs etc for action.	S.Th.
Trenches EDAN SECTOR	17/11/16	"	Batt'n left ENGLEBELMER at 11 p.m. full fighting order for trenches. Marched through "MAILLY MAILLET and passed through "WHITE CITY." Having formed into single file sometime before this point the Batt'n went across the open road by the C.O. towards trenches opposite beaver road roughly running from K.35.c.5.4 to Q.35.a.5.8. Gradually any trench leading eastwards we entered the east face of QUADRILATERAL known as North Lane. The Batt'n on the way to these trenches received much shell fire & casualties were evident. The relief again of them was from to follow. Some difficulty was experienced at 6 a.m. Commenced at 7 a.m. was completed at 9 a.m. The C.O. having looked all companies in trenches & gone round withdrew struck out about by shell fires	

WAR DIARY

Army Form C. 2118.

11th Border Regt

INTELLIGENCE SUMMARY

Place	Date	Hour	Summary of Events and Information	Remarks and references to Appendices
TRENCHES LEDAN SECTOR	13/11/16	10 p.m.	Heavy shelling continued throughout and while in support few more casualties. At 11 pm the C.O. went to Brigade Head Q. for a conference. The Battn had instructions where they were to move on their return to the R.O.Y.L.I. which explains our front line. Battr Company which reached a function in front line from Battn HQ K 35 c 16.0 towards WAGON ROAD was done over by C.O. & the position for the Coys to take up on the taped beyond was also from the tape which the Battn was to form for the attack. Ran roughly from K 35d 52 to Q 5 c 8.4. 12 noon a heavy barrage from our artillery was opened onto enemy lines, approx two minutes later to our Front lines strip on front afterwards enemy artillery replied & our Front line by his M.G. fire continued well on after dark. The C.O. informed all Company Commanders to confirm operations to them normal. The Bn's for Company to move into position on the tape was given them. Enemy Artillery bombardment still continued to play onto our line running roughly K 35 d 1.4 to 5.6 to 8.0 1-Q 6-7 and on the Sunk Track towards WHITE CITY. From Stanmore Company who had stranded with relief & left with dark were collected together everything got into Battn to take part of attack.	Apr. 6

WAR DIARY or INTELLIGENCE SUMMARY

Army Form C. 2118.

11th Border Regt

Place	Date	Hour	Summary of Events and Information	Remarks and references to Appendices
WAGON ROAD	18/11/16	10 p.m.	At 12 midnight the C.O. with adjt & left Battn Headquarters & proceeded where the Regiment was marched into position. Guides followed given every attention & instructions. By 4 a.m. C.O. Coys & at 4.10 a.m. Coys moved had finished into C.O. Coys. and at 4.10 a.m. Coys moved onto the tape being in position by 5 am. At Zero time 16.10 am the Artillery barrage opened & the Regiment advanced in perfect order to attack the first objective being by first light to set margin of the intense cold weather the Coys got but away but is certain that the leading platoons & several others got well over German trench. From this time things different to ascertain the exact location of every Coy. About 7 a.m. there was a heavy bombardment. Many of our own bursting short into 4 red stars. This was several sent signals which seemed to come from a Snipers nest in FRANK FORT TRENCH during which fire and the ground over which the attack was delivered. Soon after daylight Capt. Ross & 2/Lt Rundell were found with some 30 odd men of K.O.Y.L.I. in a trench running from Wagon Road at 9.5.b.59 to Munich trench at Q.6.a.3.9. They held up & astrong point at Q.6.a.3.9 & communication were start fighting & bombing attacks were delivered	

WAR DIARY
INTELLIGENCE SUMMARY

11th Border Regt.

Army Form C. 2118.

Place	Date	Hour	Summary of Events and Information	Remarks and references to Appendices
WAGON ROAD	18/11/16	10 p.m.	In the trench at approx Q.6.a.15.15 flanking posts were established a little further back, two Lewis Guns were placed in position commanding both flanks. This all who were left after dark & small ^(is) parties on the WAGON ROAD side of Munich trench returned. Eight having been killed whilst trying the enemy's wire to cooperation along WAGON ROAD. During 8th day & up till 10 p.m. Stretcher bearers & water continually over the top, are tended attending & bringing in wounded men. By this time left of the Battn. were so organised of WAGON ROAD & were unable to defence by them. From accounts ~~of~~ the wounded UNLT Several men got right ^(S.D.W.) through Munich trench, wounded then crawling back were continually sniped by enemy Battn. in same position. No action taken by Germans except for heavy Shrapnel & H.E. barrage. Carrying several Casualties.	
"	19/11/16		During attack and after, when men went holding onto ground taken enemy adopted several cowardly devices, such as some coming out unarmed with their hands up (when our men showed themselves to get enemy as prisoners) they (the enemy with hands up) would suddenly drop down when shot by concealed German sniper further on. A little after noon the Battn. was relieved by the ^(2)Manchester Fusrs. 8/10	

WAR DIARY or INTELLIGENCE SUMMARY

Army Form C. 2118

11th Border Regt

Place	Date	Hour	Summary of Events and Information	Remarks and references to Appendices
MAILLY MAILLET	20/11/16	10 pm	Battn remained in billets at MAILLY MAILLET	S.B.W
"	21/11/16	"	Battn in Billets. Sergt Major Johnston & Pte Dixon reported to Battn having broken through German line at MUNICH Trench from FRANKFORT Trench. Said that some of the bombs & H.L.I. Officers & men were still holding a portion of FRANKFORT Trench. Under Brigade orders a rescue on Rawley party was formed from the Border, 16th H.L.I. to assist Capt Smith's and L/ party in returning. Capt L Smith's & his and L/ party went up after dark under Capt Hamlin Tel men made to do anything considered being a great time.	S.B.W
"	22/11/16	"	Party under Capt Hamlin returned at 4.30 am. two others men from out of party managed to get through reported that Capt held & infy men still holding out. Another rescue party was formed composed of Borders & H.L.I. This went twenties near WAGON ROAD to had to say in readiness before resistance in case Capt Smith met with the Germans and tried to break through.	S.B.W

1875 Wt. W593/826 1,200,000 4/15 J.B.C. & A. A.D.S.S./Forms/C. 2118.

WAR DIARY
or
INTELLIGENCE SUMMARY

(Erase heading not required.)

Army Form C. 2118

11th Border Regt

Place	Date	Hour	Summary of Events and Information	Remarks and references to Appendices
ARQUEVES	23/11/16	10 pm	Rescue party had removed intrench's but no news. Batt'n received orders to march. At 1.25 pm Batt'n paraded & marched for ARQUEVES, arriving there at 4.30 pm. Draft of 12 men reported	SP/6
"	24/11/16	10 pm	Batt'n remained in billets in ARQUEVES.	SP/6
GEZAINCOURT	25/11/16	"	Batt'n paraded & left ARQUEVES at 9.25 am arriving GEZAINCOURT 12 am. Draft of 40 men reported as re-inforcements	SP/6
BERTEAUCOURT	26/11/16	"	Batt'n paraded & left GEZAINCOURT at 8.15 arriving BERTEAUCOURT 1 pm. Saw Batt'n march past him en route Gen. BARN'S	SP/6
"	27/11/16	"	Company parades for inspections	SP/6
"	28/11/16	"	" " instruction	SP/6
"	29/11/16	"	General parades of instruction & training	SP/6
"	30/11/16	"	" "	SP/6

Stuart F. Hughes 2/Lt
R. C. Bircham Lt Col

Vol 13

G Webb 13. P

CONFIDENTIAL.

War Diary
of
11th Border Regiment
from 1st December 1916 to 31st December 1916
(Volume 13)

Army Form C. 2118

WAR DIARY
or
INTELLIGENCE SUMMARY

(Erase heading not required.)

Instructions regarding War Diaries and Intelligence Summaries are contained in F. S. Regs., Part II. and the Staff Manual respectively. Title Pages will be prepared in manuscript.

Place	Date	Hour	Summary of Events and Information	Remarks and references to Appendices

1875 Wt. W593/826 1,000,000 4/15 J.B.C. & A. A.D.S.S./Forms/C. 2118.

Army Form C. 2118

WAR DIARY
or
INTELLIGENCE SUMMARY
(Erase heading not required.)

Instructions regarding War Diaries and Intelligence Summaries are contained in F.S. Regs., Part II. and the Staff Manual respectively. Title Pages will be prepared in manuscript.

Place	Date	Hour	Summary of Events and Information	Remarks and references to Appendices
BERTEAUCOURT	1/12/16		Training under Coy. arrangements. Same as in afternoon. Jnl.	
W.T.	2/12/16		Church Parade and inspection of Billets by C.O. Jnl.	
"	3/12/16		Training as on 1/12/16 Jnl.	
"	4/12/16		Battn. parades for Route March. Route PERNOIS - BERNEUIL - DOMART.	
"	5/12/16		Practising attack and rearguard. Jnl. Bn. Comr. in Sniping and Lewis Gun. One Coy employed in constructing Bayonetting & Listing Course. Remainder under Coy arrangements. Jnl.	
"	6/12/16		Training. One Coy under Physical drill Instructor. Second Coy Commander in Coy arrangements. Jnl. Afternoon - practising for Coy courtesy evening.	
"	7/12/16		Representing Coins under Battn arrangement. Inter party - Battn paraded to practice of Inspection by Corps Commander Major A. Moor's assumed command of Battn during Col. Sidman's absence on leave. Jnl.	
"	8/12/16		Battn. parades for Aeroplane scheme - Emeelles & Gwing Stands Jnl. Temp. Capt (acting Major) A. Moor's transferred from 17 Bn. & 11 Border Reg. with effect from 11th Oct. as Temporary Major	

1875 Wt. W593/826 1,000,000 4/15 J.B.C. & A. A.D.S.S./Forms/C. 2118.

WAR DIARY
or
INTELLIGENCE SUMMARY
(Erase heading not required.)

Army Form C. 2118

Place	Date	Hour	Summary of Events and Information	Remarks and references to Appendices
ERTEAUCOURT	9/12/16		Church Parade and Inspection of Billets by C.O. JHL	
	10/12/16		Battn. parades on Fortress Grounds at 10: am and was inspected by General Fanshaw Commanding 5th Corps. JHL	
	11/12/16		Battn. parades for Baths. JHL	
	12/12/16		Bombing under Battn. Bombing Officer. Battn. Scouts March Route under Scout Officer. All other O.O. in afternoon. JHL	
	13/12/16		HALLOY - CANAPLES: tenth under Battn. Instructors. Coy parades to without tents. JHL Bombing. Lewis Guns under Bn. Coy. arrangement. JHL Range placed at its under 13/12/16 JHL	
	14/12/16		Battn. route march - PERNOIS - BERNEUIL - DOMART. JHL	
	15/12/16		Battn. moves to billets in PUSHEVILLERS. Inspected by Brigadier Commander on march. JHL	
	16/12/16		Church Parade and inspection of Billets by C.O. JHL	
PUSHEVILLERS	17/12/16			

WAR DIARY or INTELLIGENCE SUMMARY

Army Form C. 2118

Instructions regarding War Diaries and Intelligence Summaries are contained in F.S. Regs., Part II. and the Staff Manual respectively. Title Pages will be prepared in manuscript.

(Erase heading not required.)

Place	Date	Hour	Summary of Events and Information	Remarks and references to Appendices
SHEVILLERS	18/12/16		Battn. Border park route – Battn. Bombing officers. Remainder of Battn. preparing men training prog. JWL	
"	19/12/16		As for 18/12/16. One officer per Coy attends Gas school for one day. JWL	
"	20/12/16		Men lecturing & learning Lewis Gun course. Remainder of Battn – parade for Battn. Gas exercise Co. and attend men's training prog. at 11.6 JWL	
"	21/12/16		Battn. paraded for Brig. Inst. movement – kept in army & lecturing. Lecturing usual – Coy arrangement. JWL	
"	22/12/16		Church parade – inspection of Billets. JWL	
"	23/12/16		Holy Communion at 9 a.m. and 12 noon. – Games for remainder of day. JWL	
"	24/12/16		Battn. paraded for Bde. Route March. – Inspected by General Gough Commanding 5th Army – on the march	

1875 Wt. W593/826 6,000,000 4/15 J.B.C. & A. A.D.S.S./Forms/C.2118.

WAR DIARY
or
INTELLIGENCE SUMMARY

Army Form C. 2118

Place	Date	Hour	Summary of Events and Information	Remarks and references to Appendices
BSHEVILLERS	27/12/16		Batta. had return to Batta. line - Company training and Batta. bombing thrown smoke bombs. Accident in bombing Sapper. T. Rankin (A/bombing officer) wounded and sent to hospital. JH.	
"	28/12/16		As for 27/12/16. JH.	
"	29/12/16		Per Enjoying and Mfg Riding Course - Training men coy arrangements. Lt. Col. Ridsdale D.S.O. assumes command of Batta. JH.	
"	30/12/16		Batta. knew to tactical scheme - building new foundation to attend. - Afternoon bombing etc. JH.	
"	31/12/16		Church Parade. - 150 O.R. working for tips - Ruches etc. Fitting and testing of new smoke Box Respirators. JH.	

Henry J Harper

WAR DIARY
or
INTELLIGENCE SUMMARY.
(Erase heading not required.)

Army Form C. 2118.

XI Bde

Place	Date	Hour	Summary of Events and Information	Remarks and references to Appendices
PUCHVILLERS	1/1/17	10 pm	Battn carried out General Training & bombing. Working parties supplied & General Training	S/D/6
"	2/1/17	"	" " " "	S/D/6 S/D/6
"	3/1/17	"	" " " "	S/D/6
"	4/1/17	"	Brigade Field day. Battn carried out practice "Shunt" attack moving through PUCHVILLERS attacking a unfinished junction.	
"	5/1/17	"	General training & bombing.	S/D/6
"	6/1/17	"	One company (A) left PUCHVILLERS in lorries to BUS & marched from there to CORCELLES.	
"	7/1/17	"	Battn paraded full marching order left in lorries for BUS & marched to CORCELLES arriving 3.30 pm. Army left 12 noon.	S/D/6
CORCELLES	8/1/17	"	Battn in billets CORCELLES. Supplied working parties in trenches	S/D/6
"	9/1/17	"	Gen. JARDINE visited billets. Battn supplied carrying & sinking parties in trenches.	S/D/6 C Roles
"	10/1/17	"	Battn paraded & left billets by companies relieving 14th H.L.I. in trenches C 3 Sector (SERRE).	S/D/6

14 P.
5 sheet

Army Form C. 2118.

WAR DIARY
or
INTELLIGENCE SUMMARY.
(Erase heading not required.)

Instructions regarding War Diaries and Intelligence Summaries are contained in F. S. Regs., Part II and the Staff Manual respectively. Title pages will be prepared in manuscript.

Place	Date	Hour	Summary of Events and Information	Remarks and references to Appendices
TRENCHES SUB-SECTOR C.3.	11/1/17	10 p.m.	Batt'n occupying front line with 3 Companies in front & 1 in support. Enemy fractionly shelled system of trenches.	S.A.'s
ORCELLES	12/1/17		Batt'n in line. Enemy artillery very active. At 2.30 p.m. Batt'n systematically bombarded. Trenches in rear area & communication trench Companies & Brigade cut. 4.30 p.m. enemy bombardment. During evening bombardment died down. Our artillery effectively replying. Batt'n was relieved by 14th H.L.I. & went to billets.	S.A.'s
ORCELLES	13/1/17		Batt'n in billets. Supplied working parties & when carrying parties. One Company remained at COLINCAMP in working trenches. One Company in trenches O.P. Dugouts. Batt'n paraded & marched to BUS. Except one Company at Cotcher in BUS. Supplied working parties.	S.A.
BUS.	14/1/17		" " "	S.A.
"	15/1/17		" " "	S.A.
"	16/1/17		" " "	S.A.
"	17/1/17		" " when in rains drawing	S.A.
AILLY MAILLET.	18/1/17		Batt'n left BUS at 1.45 p.m. arriving MAILLY MAILLET. 3 p.m. & went into Billets.	S.A.

Army Form C. 2118.

WAR DIARY
or
INTELLIGENCE SUMMARY.
(Erase heading not required.)

Instructions regarding War Diaries and Intelligence Summaries are contained in F.S. Regs., Part II and the Staff Manual respectively. Title pages will be prepared in manuscript.

Place	Date	Hour	Summary of Events and Information	Remarks and references to Appendices
MAILLY- MAILLET	19/1/17	10 pm	Battⁿ in Billets. One officer Jun Coy went to trenches & remained in line. C.O. & 5 other officers visited line prior to relieving 2nd Gordons.	
"	20/1/17	"	Battⁿ received instructions prior to trenches & left MAILLY-MAILLET at 3.30 pm & relieved 2nd Gordons in Section R1 (Beaumont Hamel). Battⁿ in trenches R1 Section (Beaumont Hamel D.)	
"	21/1/17	"	" " One Company in reserve Station.	
"	22/1/17	"	ROAD " " Two infantry line	
"	23/1/17	"	Battⁿ in trenches R1 Section. Point 28 hrs occupied & infant established there. Patrols sent out during night.	
LYTHAN CAMP	24/1/17	"	Battⁿ was relieved by 14th H.L.I. & proceeded to LYTHAN CAMP. P.M. a s.y.	
"	25/1/17	"	Battⁿ in LYTHAN Camp.	
"	26/1/17	"	" "	
Section R.2.	27/1/17	"	Battⁿ proceeded to BEAUMONT HAMEL & relieved 2nd R.D.F.L. in Section R.2.	

Army Form C. 2118.

WAR DIARY
or
INTELLIGENCE SUMMARY.
(Erase heading not required.)

Instructions regarding War Diaries and Intelligence Summaries are contained in F. S. Regs., Part II. and the Staff Manual respectively. Title pages will be prepared in manuscript.

Place	Date	Hour	Summary of Events and Information	Remarks and references to Appendices
R.2. Sector.	28/1/17	10 pm	Batt.n in trenches R.2 sector. During previous evening Patrols sent out to X 36 c 29 reporting enemy there	S.S.P. 10
BEAUMONT HAMEL	29/1/17	"	Batt.n in line. Relieved at 6.20 pm. by 14th H.L.I. went to dug outs in BEAUMONT HAMEL. Working parties C.O. & officers went over works (defences) of B.H.	S.S.P. 10
"	30/1/17	"	Batt.n in Dug outs BEAUMONT HAMEL. Stand to at 1 am.	S.S.P. 10
1 Scot.R.	31/1/17	"	R.1 Relieving 16th H.L.I. C.O. went up on sector for JARDINE " C.O. went to interview	S.S.P. 10

Stuart H. Huyh
O.C.

A. Goodwood Lt Col.

2353 Wt W2544/1454 700,000 5/15 D. D. & L. A.D.S.S./Forms/C. 2118.

Army Form C. 2118.

WAR DIARY
or
INTELLIGENCE SUMMARY.

(Erase heading not required.)

Instructions regarding War Diaries and Intelligence Summaries are contained in F. S. Regs., Part II. and the Staff Manual respectively. Title pages will be prepared in manuscript.

Place	Date	Hour	Summary of Events and Information	Remarks and references to Appendices

2353 Wt. W2514/1454 700,000 5/15 D. D. & L. A.D.S.S./Forms/C. 2118.

CONFIDENTIAL

WAR DIARY

of

11th BORDER REGT.

from 1st Jan to 31st Jan 1917.

(Volume 14)

Confidential.

War Diary
of
11th Border Regiment
from 1st February 1917 to 28th February 1917.
(Volume 15)

Army Form C. 2118.

WAR DIARY
or
INTELLIGENCE SUMMARY.
(Erase heading not required.)

Instructions regarding War Diaries and Intelligence Summaries are contained in F. S. Regs., Part II. and the Staff Manual respectively. Title pages will be prepared in manuscript.

Place	Date	Hour	Summary of Events and Information	Remarks and references to Appendices

2353 Wt. W3344/1454 700,000 5/15 D. D. & L. A.D.S.S./Forms/C. 2118.

Vol /5 11th Bn The Border Regt

WAR DIARY
or
INTELLIGENCE SUMMARY. 11th Bn The Border Regt.

(Erase heading not required.)

Army Form C. 2118.

Place	Date	Hour	Summary of Events and Information	Remarks and references to Appendices
SUB SECTOR R.1. BEAUMONT HAMEL	1/2/17	10 p.m.	Batt in line. Two Companys in front line, one in support, one in reserve. C.O. visited line.	S/h/o
"	2/2/17	"	Batt in line. Two patrols sent out. Enemy being discovered 8 S/h/o.	
LYTHAN CAMP (BEAUSSART)	3/2/17	"	return ref. L. 31 d. 6.3. C.O. visited posts. Batt received orders to march to LYTHAN CAMP near BEAUSSART.	S/h/o
"	4/2/17	"	Batt practical drill for an attack to take place. General practice scheme to officers. C.O. explained practice scheme and tried out to correspond to actual Batt. had 'practice drill' for attack.	S/h/o
"	5/2/17	"	morning - evening, making necessary alterations in scheme. C.O. explained practice 'stunt' in morning. C.O. took all officers + platoon Commanders up to front line explaining to each the way division	S/h/o
"	6/2/17	"	of place the Battalion would attack from. The jumping off tape also laid. Practice parade by Batt in the attack morning + evening.	S/h/o
"	7/2/17	"	Operations resumed. Take on actual ground instead of supposed.	S/h/o
"	8/2/17	"	Batt. Spent day in making necessary preparations for an attacks re-equip/age, cleaning, of bombs etc. Phantom orders? Final orders issued to Company Commanders + officers.	S/h/o

WAR DIARY
or
INTELLIGENCE SUMMARY.

Army Form C. 2118.

(Erase heading not required.)

Place	Date	Hour	Summary of Events and Information	Remarks and references to Appendices
R.1.a.5.5. Y8 SECTOR R.1. BEAUMONT HAMEL	10/2/17	11 p.m.	11th BORDER Regt. Batth paraded in full fighting order & marched to BEAUMONT HAMEL in accordance with Operation Orders. Received 4 Battalion Operation orders No 10; the 94th Infy Bde being detailed to drive the enemy off the ridge running R.11.a.8.8. to R.1.a.0.9. front of TEN TREE ALLEY on the night 10th/11th. The Batth halted at quarry in BEAUMONT HAMEL where tea and ration of rum was issued. Bombs & Lewis Gun ammunition was also issued. At 6 p.m. the first platoon being one of D Coy moved off from the Quarry. From this Snicker were left along the front & followed up the tape viz WAGON ROAD — WALKER QUARRY — to Col WALKER AVENUE across it to GOUGH POST — FRANKFORT POST. Platoons followed at an interval of 100 yds along this route. C Coy (Capt Ross) were the first to make along taking up their position but the tape on the right flank in four names viz two platoons in front forming 1st & 2nd lines, two sections of each platoon being in extended	ODb

WAR DIARY or INTELLIGENCE SUMMARY

Army Form C. 2118.

11th BORDER Regt.

Place	Date	Hour	Summary of Events and Information	Remarks and references to Appendices
R1.a.5.5 Sub Sector R1. BEAUMONT HAMEL	10/2/17	11.pm.	Continued 10/2/17. Under infront & two in rear 20 yds distance. One platoon 40 yds in rear again extended right across Company front making 3rd wave. One platoon 70 yds in rear making 4th wave. M. sections in file. B Coy (Capt WALKER) followed C Coy & took up their position on the right in same formation as Battn Centre. A Coy (Capt GREENHILL) followed B & took up their position on left in artillery formation. One platoon being in front to form right flank of C Coy to deal with enemy posts in trench R1. a. 5.3. D Coy (Lieut HARRIS) with two platoons close up in rear of right flank of C Coy to deal with enemy posts in trench R1. a. 5.3. & two platoons close in rear of left flank to deal with one platoon as Battn Reserve in artillery formation. The Battn was in position at 4.30 pm & H.Q. being established at FRANKFORT hut. Battn frontage being 350 yards. Zero time 5.30 pm, in which artillery barrage opened.	[signature]

WAR DIARY
or
INTELLIGENCE SUMMARY.

(Erase heading not required.)

Army Form C. 2118.

Summary of Events and Information 11th Bn. The BORDER Regt.

Place	Date	Hour		Remarks and references to Appendices

R.1.a.5.5.
July 1st
1916.
BEAUMONT HAMEL.

Continued 10/11.

Opened up. On the Barrage commencing the Battn advanced from their position being close running from front S. of Frankfort past to KYLE and closely followed the Creeping Barrage towards their objective a line running from R.1. a.5.6. through R.1. a.5.8. to L.31. c.5.3. to first posts along our front of that line. The men behaved splendidly & kept well up with the barrage right on to their objective. The first message was sent from the reserve Coy at 9.30 to say all objectives had been captured & consolidation begun. Our left flank was exposed & had to be thrown back. The 2nd R.O.G.L.R. which was on the left flank had one company not yet up into position on our immediate left. As the time of advance commencing Bath moved off with his flank exposed. The first batch of 35 prisoners was sent back soon after being taken. The C.O. Lt. Col. GIRDWOOD moved this H.Q. forward to line R.1. a.5.5. He then examined round won & his prisoners & troops sending two prisoners

[signature]

Army Form C. 2118.

WAR DIARY
or
INTELLIGENCE SUMMARY.
(Erase heading not required.)

Summary of Events and Information 11th Bn. The BORDER Regt

Place	Date	Hour		Remarks and references to Appendices
			Continued 10/11/17	
R.1.9.5.5	10/11/17	10pm	Offensive Coy D manoeuvred across to the exposed left flank. Posts were established in front of captured tnl Gun Pit trench & reorganised out to front [illegible] to man into state of defence. Two officers & approx 100 O.R. were captured by the Battalion & sent back as prisoners of war. The enemy not in contact, the enemy tried by flares to code out and was bombed unfortunately. Orgt for the enemy trench finding. Patrols from Coy S were pushed out & also patrols sent to try & establish communication with 1st KOYLI. A strong by held enemy post was discovered at on British left flank. Two Vickers were sent along by C.O. under the orders Stokes Morton detachment under Lieut. Sincocles were now sent along to that flank. The Stokes mortar opened up onto hostile post.	
Pt a 35 Sub Sector R.1 BEAUMONT HAMEL	11/2/17	10 pm	At 4.30 am enemy delivered a counter attack from N.E. direction. Rapid rifle fire was thought to [illegible]	

WAR DIARY or INTELLIGENCE SUMMARY

Place	Date	Hour	Summary of Events and Information 1/1st Bn The BORDER Regt.	Remarks and references to Appendices
P.1.a.5.5.	11/2/17	10 p.m.	Continued. Remainder of day quiet with exception of hostile sniping and occasional active artillery fire. two attempts by the eny on the left turn much to capture the strong shell hole post near that flank. Both attempts were unsuccessful owing to the post being two strongly held. At 8.30 p.m. orders were received that the Battn that post was to act in conjunction with the 1st Manc Borderers in another advance to be made along our right on the PUISIEUX ridge. D Coy was detailed. They took up their position on the left flank of the 1st Manc Borderers + the barrage opening up at 9 p.m. the regiment started some 300 yds. beyond being taken the Battn held. A new line of posts was established connecting up with the 1st Manc Borderers,	Sgd [initials] /o

WAR DIARY or INTELLIGENCE SUMMARY

Army Form C. 2118.

Place	Date	Hour	Summary of Events and Information 11th Bn the BORDER Regt	Remarks and references to Appendices
R.1. a.55 Sub Sector R1 BEAUMONT HAMEL	Continued 11th		In conjunction with Lewis & Vickers Gun fire onto enemy the hostile attack was shelled off with the exception of our left flank. Under cover of burning the smoke from the flaming dugout he managed to get up to our lines. A fight then ensued with bombs enemy which the enemy was repulsed mainly the arm ground by smoke was emptied by rifle volleys. Injury and barrage with all available rifle grenades. An S O S signal for artillery was sent up. Soon after the artillery opened up a hurricane of attack was completely broken. The enemy beating into valley & many of apparente taking observation was employed going to heavy mist. A daylight patrol went out found enemy still members on left flank throwing a front with their M.G.'s. Then must cloud visibility was good several new shots who could be seen retiring up could be sniped. Both rifle & Lewis Gun fire with good effect then bright on to parties throwing away of enemy	J.J.B.

Army Form C. 2118.

WAR DIARY
or
INTELLIGENCE SUMMARY.
(Erase heading not required.)

Instructions regarding War Diaries and Intelligence Summaries are contained in F. S. Regs., Part II. and the Staff Manual respectively. Title pages will be prepared in manuscript.

11th Bn. The Border Regt.

Place	Date	Hour	Summary of Events and Information	Remarks and references to Appendices
BEAUMONT HAMEL	12/2/17	10 p.m.	The Battn was relieved by 16th H.L.I. relief being completed at 4 a.m. the Battn withdrew to dug outs on STATION ROAD BEAUMONT HAMEL & dug outs nr the Y ravine.	S/B/10
	13/2/17	"	Battn in dug outs STATION ROAD & Y ravine.	
	14/2/17	"	" The 32nd Division being relieved by 62nd Divn	S/B/10
ACHEUX	15/2/17	"	Battn withdrew to Acheux.	S/B/10
"	16/2/17	"	Battn remained in huts at ACHEUX.	S/B/10
"	17/2/17	"	"	S/B/10
MIRVAUX	18/2/17	"	Battn handed full marching order. left ACHEUX 8.30 am arriving MIRVAUX 1 p.m.	S/B/10
"	19/2/17	"	Battn remained in MIRVAUX. General parades for training & inspection	S/B/10
"	20/2/17	"	" "	S/B/10
CAMON	21/2/17	"	Battn paraded full marching order & marched to CAMON.	S/B/10
AMIEN	22/2/17	"	" " WEINCOURT.	S/B/10
WEINCOURT	23/2/17	"	Battn remained in WEINCOURT. General parades for training &c	S/B/W
"	24/2/17	"	" "	S/B/

Army Form C. 2118.

WAR DIARY
or
INTELLIGENCE SUMMARY.
(Erase heading not required.)

Instructions regarding War Diaries and Intelligence Summaries are contained in F. S. Regs., Part II. and the Staff Manual respectively. Title pages will be prepared in manuscript.

Summary of Events and Information 11th Bn. The BORDER Regt

Place	Date	Hour	Summary of Events and Information	Remarks and references to Appendices
	25/2/19	10/pm	Batt'n paraded full marching order & left for QUESNEL. Leaving 12.30pm arriving 4.15 pm.	S&b
QUESNEL	26/2/19	"	Batt'n remained in QUESNEL. General parades for inspection & improvement of billets.	S&b
"	27/2/19	"	General parades for training & instruction.	S&b
"	28/2/19	"	Batt'n paraded full marching order for Bn Brigade inspection by Divisional Commander.	S&b

Shan L Duff
Lieut
9. O. 11th Border Regt.

B Garland Lt Col
a/g 11 Border Regt

CONFIDENTIAL.

War Diary
of
11th Border Regiment
From 1st March 1917 to 31st March 1917
(Volume 16).

Army Form C. 2118.

WAR DIARY
or
INTELLIGENCE SUMMARY.

(*Erase heading not required.*)

Instructions regarding War Diaries and Intelligence Summaries are contained in F. S. Regs., Part II. and the Staff Manual respectively. Title pages will be prepared in manuscript.

Place	Date	Hour	Summary of Events and Information	Remarks and references to Appendices

2353 Wt. W2544/-454 700,000 5/15 D. D. & L. A.D.S.S./Forms/C.2118.

Army Form C. 2118.

WAR DIARY
or
INTELLIGENCE SUMMARY.

11th Bn The Border Regt
B.E.F. France
Vol 16

(Erase heading not required.)

16 P.
5 sheets

Place	Date	Hour	Summary of Events and Information	Remarks and references to Appendices
LE QUESNEL	1/3/17	10 pm	Batt'n in billets at LE QUESNEL as Brigade Reserve. Preparations being made prior to marching to Line. At 1 pm Batt'n paraded & moved off by companies to relieved 9nd R.S.R. 11th in Support line KUROPATKIN. Major Chamberlayne joined the Batt'n & took over as second in command.	S.A.6
KUROPATKIN	2/3/17	10 pm	Batt'n as Support in the Intermediate Line (KUROPATKIN) working parties on trenches.	S&6
"	3/3/17	"	R E working parties supplied, also improvement & clearing out of trenches.	S&6
"	4/3/17	"	Ditto	S&6
EY SECTOR	5/3/17	"	Batt'n went into front line System & relieved 17th H.L.I. relief complete 11 p.m. Slight activity of enemy with T.Ms & aerial Darts.	S&6
HUGUERSCOURT	6/3/17	"	Batt'n in line. Patrols sent out. Clearing of trenches carried on.	S&6
"	7/3/17	"	"	S&6
"	8/3/17	"	Batt'n was relieved by 14th H.L.I. & withdrew to KUROPATKIN as Support.	S&6

Army Form C. 2118.

WAR DIARY
or
INTELLIGENCE SUMMARY. 1/4 The BORDER REGT
(Erase heading not required.)

Place	Date	Hour	Summary of Events and Information	Remarks and references to Appendices
MOPATKIN.	9/3/17	10/pm	Batt. in Support Intermediate line. Working parties for R.E. Discussion for proposed Raid on Enemy Trench.	S&h
"	10/3/17	"	Raid decided on & party of volunteers chosen. Party of 160 withdrawn out of line to BEAUCOURT to practice for Raid	S&h
"	11/3/17	"	Batt. & R.E. working parties in trenches	S&h
E/ SECTOR	12/3/17	"	Batt. & R.E. working parties during day. Batt. relieved 14th H.L.I. in front the trenches.	S&h
	13/3/17	"	Batt. holding front line. Patrols sent out. Preparations made for Raid	S&h
	14/3/17	"	Batt. was relieved by 14 M.H.L.I. relief complete	S&h
		3.15 am	Batt. lost one patrol of Sergt & two men taken prisoners.	
E QUEENEK	15/3/17	"	Working parties supplied. Batt. spent day in general clean up	S&h
	16/3/17	"	Batt. in Brigade in reserve. Parades of training & working parties.	S&h
ROSSIGNOY	17/3/17	"	Retirement of German army. The Division moved forward. Batt. paraded in fighting order & marched to ROUVROY remaining S&h there the night.	S&h

Army Form C. 2118.

WAR DIARY
or
INTELLIGENCE SUMMARY. 11th Bn. Th. BORDER Regt.
(Erase heading not required.)

Place	Date	Hour	Summary of Events and Information	Remarks and references to Appendices
ATTENCOURT	18/3/17	10 pm	The German continued his retirement followed by French on Division's right. Division moved forward two Brigades in front one in Reserve. Battn moved to old German Front line South of FOUQUESCOURT. Worked on Roads stopped trenches to allow Artillery & Transport to pass. At 3.30 pm Battn moved forward to HATTENCOURT remained in night.	S.A.6
HERLEY	19/3/17	10 pm	Division continued its advance & Battn marched to HERLEY which was completely destroyed by retiring enemy. Battn remained there overnight.	S.A.6
NESLE	20/3/17	10 pm	Battn marched to NESLE leaving HERLEY 9 am & arrived in NESLE 11 am filled there.	S.A.6
"	21/3/17 "		Battn remained in NESLE. Working parties on roads & bridges destroyed by enemy. Craters on Cross roads filled in.	S.A.6
"	22/3/17 "		Working parties on Bridges roads etc. Guards & piquets supplied. Remainder Battn sapper Batted.	S.A.6
"	23/3/17 "		Battn marched to friends WEST of Roy & there dug strong points. i.e. the Ground in front was marked out.	S.A.6
"	24/3/17 "		Battn marched & marched to Ground WEST of ROY & there dug strong points. Each Company digging one of 32 of the Tray S.	S.A.6

WAR DIARY or INTELLIGENCE SUMMARY. 1/4 Bn The Border Regt

Army Form C. 2118.

Place	Date	Hour	Summary of Events and Information	Remarks and references to Appendices
NESLE.	25/3/17	10 p.m.	Battn all but one company paraded & marched to dig on strong points.	S.A.6
"	26/3/17	"	Ditto.	S.A.6
"	27/3/17	"	Battn supplied R.E. working parties on Roads & Bridges.	S.A.6
FORESTE.	28/3/17	"	Battn paraded & marched East leaving NESLE 12.0 am. passed through VOYENNES to TUGNY arriving there 3.30 p.m. at 6 & 8. Battn continued march to FRIERES halted for 3 hrs. Dug Trenches 400 yds frontage facing Eastwards. NORTH OF GERMAINE	S.A.6
"	29/3/17	"	Battn rested during day & continued digging during night. One company dug out posts at VAUX & another at ETREILLERS. (Ref Map. Sheet 66D in St QUENTIN.)	S.A.6
"	30/3/17	"	Battn remained in Billets during day. Orders received that Battn would attack the village of SAVY Operation Orders issued for attack.	S.A.6
"	31/3/17	"		

Stuart D Wolff
Lt/Col
J.O. XI Border Regt

A Ginkard LCC
C.O. 1/4 Border Regt

CONFIDENTIAL.

War Diary

of

1st Border Regiment

from 1st April 1917 to 30th April 1917.

(Volume 17)

Army Form C. 2118.

WAR DIARY
or
INTELLIGENCE SUMMARY.
(Erase heading not required.)

Instructions regarding War Diaries and Intelligence Summaries are contained in F. S. Regs., Part II. and the Staff Manual respectively. Title pages will be prepared in manuscript.

Place	Date	Hour	Summary of Events and Information	Remarks and references to Appendices

2353 Wt. W2544/f454 700,000 5/15 D. D. & L. A.D.S.S./Forms/C. 2118.

WAR DIARY or INTELLIGENCE SUMMARY

11th Bn. The Border Regt.

Army Form C. 2118.

Place	Date	Hour	Summary of Events and Information	Remarks and references to Appendices
SAVY	1/4/17	10 p.m.	On the night 31/3/1st the Battn moved forward from FORESTE onto the ROBY ~~ESTRÉES~~ JEFFREUILLES road. The 7th and 8th Infantry Brigades on right. At 3:30 am Battn halted here & a ration of rum was issued. 500 yds S.W. of the village moved forward 1700 yds to position & took up formation into attacking formation & took up attacking position. At 5 am the artillery barrage opened. Then it extended along previously laid tape. The Battn moved forward to the attack barrage opening up. The Battn moved forward with all possible speed on SAVY. The Battn moved forward through and past behind the barrage & drove the enemy before them upon the village + dug in on the opposite side with the exception of one company which remained in the village to mop it up. Any concealed enemy. Several prisoners were taken & numbers of the enemy killed. The capture of the village was practically complete. By 6:30 am all consolidation was started. Battn in a state of defence. Later on the Battn also took over the line held by the 14th H.L.I. who withdrew. During afternoon from 2:30 - 3:30 pm enemy heavily shelled our positions. Battn worked on defences all day.	Not much [illegible] taken about 30 – rifles. 4/5. [signature] Surdell 17 P. 6 about S.8.6

WAR DIARY
INTELLIGENCE SUMMARY. 11th Bn. The Border Regt.

Army Form C. 2118.

Place	Date	Hour	Summary of Events and Information	Remarks and references to Appendices
SAVY	2/4/17	10 p.m.	Battn. remained in defences around SAVY, working parties all day on village. Salvage of material, collecting of eng. etc. Clearing defences. Clearing ground & through village. Improvement on defences.	SDK
"	3/4/17	"	Salvage, collection of wood, working parties on village. Clearing ground. Working parties also supplied observers. Gas Companies sent in Bois de Holnon. Digging outposts.	SDK
"	4/4/17	"	Working parties in ETREILLERS also working parties during night. T.C.O. of Companies went forward & reconnoitred ground, enemy lines also outings of Holnon.	SDK
"	5/4/17	"	Battn. remained in Savy. Working parties, also during night.	SDK
"	6/4/17	"	" " " "	SDK
"	7/4/17	"	Battn left SAVY 8 p.m. arriving HOLNON 9.30. Dug shelters remained as support to two Battns. in front.	SDK
HOLNON	8/4/17	"	Work done on shelters & position.	DK
"	9/4/17	"	Remained as support to two Battns. in front-line. One Coy immediate support to 17 & 21. Work done on shelters etc.	[signature]

Army Form C. 2118.

WAR DIARY
or
INTELLIGENCE SUMMARY.
(Erase heading not required.)

11th Bn. The Border Regt.

Instructions regarding War Diaries and Intelligence Summaries are contained in F.S. Regs., Part II. and the Staff Manual respectively. Title pages will be prepared in manuscript.

Place	Date	Hour	Summary of Events and Information	Remarks and references to Appendices
HOLNON	10/4/17	10 pm	Batt. (less one Coy) remained in support to two Battns. in front line. Improving. Artillery etc. Commenced relief of 11th K.L.I. from in front line from M.33 south to S.15 (?). Relief complete 10.20 pm.	
HOLNON	11/4/17	10 pm	Batt. in front line. Improving trenches, fire positions & communication trenches. Reconnaissance of ground in front.	
HOLNON	12/4/17	10 pm	Batt. remained in front line. Improving positions etc.	
HOLNON	13/4/17	10 pm	Batt. remained in front line. do do do.	
HOLNON	14/4/17	10 pm	on FAYET. Assault by 2nd K.O.Y.L.I. + 6th H.L.I. Commenced 4.30 am. Batt. remained in line ready to concentrate if ordered. Artillery opened up barrage at 1.10 pm and Batt. advanced on objective in extended order. At 1.26 pm Batt. reached sunken road. M.28.c & M.34.b. A.M.G. opened fire from left front & inflicted several casualties to the left flank of the leading Coy. Two platoons of the reserve Coy were ordered up to deal with it at 1.33 pm. In this they were successful & captured the gun complete. A telephone line from was run out to Batt. at 1.30 pm & communicating authorities	Map 62 b. S.W. 1/20000

NIFFMT

WAR DIARY
or
INTELLIGENCE SUMMARY

Army Form C. 2118.

11th Batta. The Border Regt.

Place	Date	Hour	Summary of Events and Information	Remarks and references to Appendices
				Map G2b-SW
N. St FAYET	14-4-17	1.15 pm	A report was received at 1.15 pm to the effect that the right Coy had attained their objectives and were consolidating. By 2/pm all Coys were consolidating their line. Left Coy in M28b. Left Centre Coy in M25d & M29b. Right Centre Coy in M28b. M29c along eastern edge of copse. Right Coy in M29c & M35a. Touch was established on the left with the 17th K.L.R, who were in GRICOURT. Except for slight shelling about M28d & M29c, the situation assumed special Work was carried on all night upon defences.	
N. St FAYET	15-4-17	10 pm	Batta remained in line strengthening defences etc. Relief of Batta by 16th L.F.S & 16th N.F. commenced 8.30 pm.	
GERMAINE	16-4-17	10 am	Relief complete at 11.30 pm. Batta marched to GERMAINE via HOENON, SAVY, ETREILLERS and VAUX & arrived at 5.0 am. Cleaning equipments, clothes etc.	
GERMAINE	17-4-17	10 pm	Cleaning up generally. Leaving nest clothing etc	
GERMAINE	18-4-17	10 pm	do do do	
GERMAINE	19-4-17	10 pm	Batta moved at 1.0 pm to HOMBLEUX via DOUILLY - TOULE - OFFOY arriving at 4.30 pm.	

Army Form C. 2118.

WAR DIARY
or
INTELLIGENCE SUMMARY.

(Erase heading not required.)

11th Battⁿ The Border Reg^t

Place	Date	Hour	Summary of Events and Information	Remarks and references to Appendices
HOMBLEUX	20/4/17	10 p.m.	Battⁿ occupied day by physical - platoon + company drill. Training of specialists	
HOMBLEUX	21/4/17	"	Battⁿ training, recreation	
HOMBLEUX	22/4/17	"	Church parade at 9.30 am. Presentation of Military Medal ribbon by Bde Commander (Lt. Col Eustwood D.S.O.) at 11.00 am.	
HOMBLEUX	23/4/17	"	Battⁿ route march toward Ham on tactical exercise. Huebility in afternoon	
OFFOY	24/4/17	"	Battⁿ moved from HOMBLEUX to OFFOY [ISC (60py/coy)]	
OFFOY	25/4/17	"	Battⁿ training, squaretting up generally. Draft of 91 OR arrived from I.B.D.	
OFFOY	26/4/17	"	do. Gas demonstration by Divisional Gas officer in afternoon. 12 hungary Medals awarded for operations N.E. of PUISIEUX - 14-4-17.	
OFFOY	27/4/17	"	Baths at VOYENNES for Battⁿ, occupied all day.	
OFFOY	28/4/17	"	Preliminary parades for Corps Commanders inspection. Training	
OFFOY	29/4/17	"	Preliminary parade for Battⁿ Commanders inspection - recreation. Three Military Crosses awarded for operations at SAVY-1-4-17.	
OFFOY	30/4/17	"	Brigade parade for inspection by Divisional Commander. B.C. compliments for good work in recent operations.	

Wrallythwaite
Intelligence Officer
11th Border Reg^t

A Chamberlayne ?
Lt Col
11 Bord^r Reg^t

CONFIDENTIAL

War Diary
of
11th Border Regiment
from 1st May 1917 to 31st May, 1917.
(Volume 18).

Army Form C. 2118.

WAR DIARY
or
INTELLIGENCE SUMMARY.

(Erase heading not required.)

Instructions regarding War Diaries and Intelligence Summaries are contained in F. S. Regs., Part II. and the Staff Manual respectively. Title pages will be prepared in manuscript.

Place	Date	Hour	Summary of Events and Information	Remarks and references to Appendices

A5834 Wt. W4973/M687 750,000 8/16 D. D. & L. Ltd. Forms/C.2118/13.

WAR DIARY
or
INTELLIGENCE SUMMARY.
(Erase heading not required.)

Army Form C. 2118.

11th Batt. The Border Regt.

Place	Date	Hour	Summary of Events and Information	Remarks and references to Appendices
OFFOY	1/5/17	10am	Company + Batt. drill. Training generally.	
OFFOY	2/5/17	"	Inspection of Brigade by Corps Commander. Lt. Gen. WOOLCOMBE D.S.O. Brigade praised for good work in recent operations. Exceptionally smart turn-out.	
OFFOY	3/5/17	"	Batt. drill — attack formations. Military Cross for work during operations on April 14th N.E. of Gouzet awarded BAR to S.O. & L/t. MACKAY-M.MARTIN (Tarn Copses).	
OFFOY	4/5/17	"	Route march to TOUL & DOUNS with advance + flank guards. Demonstration by 86th & 94th Trench Mortar Batteries at 3 p.m. all officers and a large percentage of men attended.	
OFFOY	5/5/17	"	Batt. drill — outpost scheme.	
OFFOY	6/5/17	"	Church Parade at 9.30 am. Drill + training generally. Recreation etc.	
OFFOY	7/5/17	"	Batt. drill at 9am.	
OFFOY	8/5/17	"	Parades cancelled owing to rain. Recreation and sports (football) in afternoon & evening.	
OFFOY	9/5/17	"	Physical training etc. Training continued in Lewis machine gun, bayonet fighting, Battalion drill + training.	
OFFOY	10/5/17	"	" route march + tactical scheme towards MATIGNY and Y.	
OFFOY	11/5/17	"	" drill — attack formation — inspects by Brigadier.	

Army Form C. 2118.

WAR DIARY
or
INTELLIGENCE SUMMARY.
(Erase heading not required.)

11th Battⁿ 1st Border Regt.

Place	Date	Hour	Summary of Events and Information	Remarks and references to Appendices
OFFOY	12-5-17	10 pm	Battⁿ in Attack formation for inspection by G.O.C. 32nd Div. Recreation in afternoon.	
OFFOY	13-5-17	10:30 am	Church parade 10 am. Staff ride under C.O. Conference in afternoon with Brigadier General BLACKLOCK D.S.O. on work in general.	
OFFOY	14-5-17	"	Brigade attack scheme. Fired 10 am. Lloyd objective taken at 11:30 am. Afternoon spent in preparation for following day's march.	
PUZEAUX	15-5-17	"	Left OFFOY 4:15 am marched to PUZEAUX via NESLE and CURCHY. Arrived 8:45 am.	
CAIX	16-5-17	"	Left PUZEAUX 5:10 am marched to CAIX via ROSIERES. Arrived 9 am. Resting.	
DOMART s/la Luce	17-5-17	"	Left CAIX at 5:40 am marched to DOMART s/la Luce. Arrived 9 am. Resting.	
DOMART	18-5-17	"	Cleaning up billets & making improvements.	
DOMART	19-5-17	"	Bath. Training & recreation.	
DOMART	20-5-17	"	Church parade & presentation of Military Medals by Lt Col GIRDWOOD D.S.O. Cmdg Battⁿ.	
DOMART	21-5-17	"	Bath. Evening & recreation.	
DOMART	22-5-17	"	do — do — do	
DOMART	23-5-17	"	do — do — do	
DOMART	24-5-17	"	do — do — do	
DOMART	25-5-17	"	do — do — do	

WAR DIARY
or
INTELLIGENCE SUMMARY.

(Erase heading not required.)

Army Form C. 2118.

11th Batt
K. Border Regt.

Place	Date	Hour	Summary of Events and Information	Remarks and references to Appendices
DOMART / EOCLE	26-5-17	10/a.m.	Bath. Training – games – recreation & Route march.	
DOMART	27.5.17	"	" Church Parade	
DOMART	28-5-17	"	Bath. training – recreation.	
DOMART	29/5/17	"	Battn. training – Divisional band inspection Batn. Training.	
VILLERS BRETONNEUX	30/5/17	"	Batn. marches to VILLERS BRETONNEUX & took on beek.	
ditto	31/5/17	"	Batn. at VILLERS BRETONNEUX – preparing to attack.	

Whittam Capt.

A Sutton Col
O.C. 11th Bord Regt

CONFIDENTIAL.

War Diary
of
11th Border Regiment
from 1st June 1917 to 30th June 1917
(Volume 19).

Army Form C. 2118.

WAR DIARY
or
INTELLIGENCE SUMMARY.

(Erase heading not required.)

Instructions regarding War Diaries and Intelligence Summaries are contained in F. S. Regs., Part II and the Staff Manual respectively. Title pages will be prepared in manuscript.

Place	Date	Hour	Summary of Events and Information	Remarks and references to Appendices

Army Form C. 2118.

WAR DIARY
or
INTELLIGENCE SUMMARY. 11th Border Regiment.
(Erase heading not required.)

Vol 19

Place	Date	Hour	Summary of Events and Information	Remarks and references to Appendices
LLERS- OTTONEUX	1-6-19	10 pm	Reveille 3 am. Battn (less on fatigue) commenced entraining at 4.45 am. Train left at 5.45 a.m. route to STEENBECQUE via ABBEVILLE - ETAPLES - BOULOGNE - CALAIS - HAZEBROUCK and arrived STEENBECQUE at 4 pm. Commenced to march to NEUF BERQUIN - DOULIEU AREA at 5 pm. VIA MERVILLE arriving 11 pm.	
EUF- BERQUIN	2-6-19	"	Battn remained in billets resting, cleaning up generally.	
EUF- BERQUIN	3-6-19	"	do do do do do	
EUF- BERQUIN	4-6-19	"	Battn on physical exercise before 8 am - training in musketry, fire control etc during morning.	
EUF- BERQUIN	5-6-19	"	do do do do Inspection of billets by Div Commdr Maj. General STUART-WORTLEY in morning.	
EUF- BERQUIN	6-6-19	"	Battn on physical exercise before breakfast. General training in musketry fire control & handling of men by Junior N.C.Os. Afternoon C.Os conference for Officers.	

Macnaughton 2/Lieut,

19 P

Army Form C. 2118.

WAR DIARY
or
INTELLIGENCE SUMMARY.
(Erase heading not required.)

Unit 4th Borden Regiment. No. 36 A.

Instructions regarding War Diaries and Intelligence Summaries are contained in F. S. Regs., Part II. and the Staff Manual respectively. Title pages will be prepared in manuscript.

Place	Date	Hour	Summary of Events and Information	Remarks and references to Appendices
NEUF-BERQUIN	7-6-17	10 pm	Battn about to in billets ready to move up to reinforce 2nd Anzac Corps in attack on OOSTAVERNE Line.	
NEUF-BERQUIN	8-6-17	"	Battn standing to.	
N. BERQUIN	9-6-17	"	Battn continued training near billets. Recreation & Musketry competition in Afternoon	
"	10-6-17	"	Battn Church parade at 11-15 am.	
"	11-6-17	"	Battn training. Recreation etc.	
"	12-6-17	"	Battn route march of 8 miles. Recreation etc.	
"	13-6-17	"	Battn training etc.	
"	14-6-17	"	Reveille 4-45 am Battn moved off at 7-12 am to GODWAERSVELDT via CAESTRE. arriving 11-30 am.	
DWAERSVELDT	15-6-17	"	Boys at disposal of Coy Commdrs for Inspection etc.	
"	16-6-17	"	Reveille 3 am. Battn marched to Broca & entrained at 9 am proceeded to ST POL. S/M. near DUNKERQUE arriving at 1 pm.	
POL. S/M.	17-6-17	"	Church parade at 10 am.	
POL. S/M.	18-6-17	"	Battn marched to sands north of MARDYCK. for attack practice & Bathing	

WAR DIARY
or
INTELLIGENCE SUMMARY.
(Erase heading not required.)

Army Form C. 2118.

Mc Bath
The Border Regt.

Instructions regarding War Diaries and Intelligence Summaries are contained in F.S. Regs., Part II. and the Staff Manual respectively. Title pages will be prepared in manuscript.

Place	Date	Hour	Summary of Events and Information	Remarks and references to Appendices
COXYDE	19-6-17	10 pm	Batt. entrained at DUNKERQUE at 11am. Detrained at COXYDE at 1.30 pm & marched to Camp JEAN BART in Sand Dunes	
COSTE- DUNKERQUE	20-6-17	"	Batt. marched from COXYDE at 6am to COSTE-DUNKERQUE arriving at Camp GALLIMARD 9.30 am.	
"	21-6-17	"	Batt. training under Coy comdr. Recreation.	
"	22-6-17	"	do — do — do	
"	23-6-17	"	do — do — do	
"	24-6-17	"	Church parade in sand dunes at 10 am. Pcol shooting in afternoon.	
"	25-6-17	"	Working parties totaling 157 found for various works. Remainder of day spent strong- hand from Camp GALLIMARD to CAMP RIBIALLET at 9.30 pm	
"	26-6-17	"	Moved from Camp RIBIALLET to NEW TRENCH & PARADE at 8.30 pm. NIEUPORT	
"	27-6-17	"	Working parties up to line during night. Strengthening & repairing trenchworks	
"	28-6-17	"	Working parties up in line during night. Continued to build O.P.	
"	29-6-17	"	Commenced to relieve 17th H.L.I. at 10 pm. Relief complete 12.50 am	
"	30-6-17	"	Patrol executed since in M.22.B&6. Day exceptionally quiet.	

CONFIDENTIAL

WAR DIARY

of the

11th Battn. THE BORDER REGT.

1st to 31st July
- 1917 -

CONFIDENTIAL.

War Diary,
of.
11th Border Regiment
From 1st July 1917 to 31st July 1917.
(Volume 20)

Army Form C. 2118.

WAR DIARY
or
INTELLIGENCE SUMMARY.

(Erase heading not required.)

Instructions regarding War Diaries and Intelligence Summaries are contained in F. S. Regs., Part II. and the Staff Manual respectively. Title pages will be prepared in manuscript.

Place	Date	Hour	Summary of Events and Information	Remarks and references to Appendices

(A7092) Wt. W23839/M1293 75,000. 1/17. D. D. & L., Ltd. Forms/C.2118/14.

Army Form C. 2118.

1st Batt.
The Border Regt

WAR DIARY
or
INTELLIGENCE SUMMARY.
(Erase heading not required.)

Place	Date	Hour	Summary of Events and Information	Remarks and references to Appendices
NIEUPORT – 1 Coy B.HQ A2/B/DE S.P. C.O.R.	1-7-17	10 p.m.	The Battalion remained in occupation of the "C" subsector. Two Companies in front line. Viz 1 2nd & 3rd Lines, 2 Coys in support. The day was moderately quiet. PONT PONTZ was shelled during morning. None was also shelled about. Enemy very inactive, except for shelling.	
"	2-7-17	10 p.m.	Battalion remained in occupation of "C" subsector. Day fairly quiet – not much shelling.	
"	3-7-17	10 p.m.	Battalion still in line. Fairly heavy shelling of left communication tunnel & PONT PASTRE which was hit in two or three places. Remainder of day quiet.	
"	4-7-17	10 p.m.	Battalion in line. Relief by 1st K.R.R.s commenced at 9 p.m. and completed by 10.30 p.m.	
"	5-7-17	10 p.m.	Battalion moved back to dugouts in thin Forest road (Reserve). At 11.24 p.m. 4-7-17 one 2/Lt PIGOTT. & 35 O.R. launched a raid on the enemy's line, consisting of Lts SYMES M.C. (wounded) /LT HERNIE/, 2/Lt PIGOTT. & 35 O.R. A Bangalore torpedo was fired at 12-15 a.m. & upon this party rushing forward they were met by a heavy barrage of bombs from the enemy. Finding the trench held too strongly and the party becoming surrounded by counselling they had to withdraw. This was done successfully, all the party returning except one killed, one missing (believed killed) one and a gunshot minute after asking for support enemy barrage at 12.26 a.m. Our artillery opened up a communication to Battery was by Lamp (Lucas Daylight) from front line to O.P. & thence by phone. Casualties in No. 2/17	

WAR DIARY
or
INTELLIGENCE SUMMARY.

(Erase heading not required.)

Army Form C. 2118.

1st Battalion
The Border Regt.

Place	Date	Hour	Summary of Events and Information	Remarks and references to Appendices
NIEUPORT	5/7/17	10 pm	Battalion in reserve. 3 Coys & 3 platoons on work forward at 10pm. 1 platoon as garrison.	JM
"	6/7/17	10 pm	2/Lt. Bishop killed on working party about midnight. 5% & Lay mount enemy M.G fire. Back areas strongely/heavily shelled during morning and afternoon with 8" naval shells. Retaliation from our field gun batteries on M15a. Enemy aeroplanes active at night.	JM
"	7/7/17	10 pm	Slight shelling of our area at 6.00 am. Enemy aerial activity in evening morning. Shelling sharply heavier during afternoon and evening. Several casualties. About 5 fast minute – 8" shells. Night much quieter.	JM
"	8/7/17	10 pm	Battalion moved into line to relieve 17th & 29 at 9.30 pm. Relief complete 11 pm. Night quiet.	JM
"	9/7/17	10 pm	Day fairly quiet. About 11.30 pm H.E. bombardment of our O.P's commenced, and lasted for about one hour. Our line signallers all O.K.	JM

J.M. Wayhart Lt.Col
C.O. 1st Border Regt.

Army Form C. 2118.

WAR DIARY
or
INTELLIGENCE SUMMARY.

(Erase heading not required.)

11th Batt
Lt Col Bower Regt

Place	Date	Hour	Summary of Events and Information	Remarks and references to Appendices

NIEUPORT. S.W.4 -OMBARTZYDE	10/7/17	10 p.m.	Composition of Battalion on morning of July 10th 1917. Batt. Head-Quarters. C.O. Lt.Col. A.C. GIRDWOOD D.S.O. Second in Command T/Capt. J.S. LOWTHIAN M.C. Adjutant 2/Lt. T.H. HODGKINSON. Asst/Adjt. 2/Lt. COOK-GRAY. Intelligence Officer. 2/Lt. J. MALLEY-MARTIN M.C. Bombing Officer 2/Lt. GILLESPIE. Signalling Officer 1/2/Lt J. JAMIE. M.O. Capt. ANDERSON R.A.M.C. Chaplain Capt. C. LANGDON. Artillery Liason Officer 2/Lt CORE Battery R.F.A.
			
			O.C. "A" Coy. T/Capt. A.E. GREENHILL. M.C. O.C. "B" Coy. T/Capt. C.H. WALKER M.C.
			         2/Lt. W.C.H. LANE. 2/Lt M. SMYTHE.
			         1/2/Lt R.E. PIGOTT. 1/2/Lt A.G. SHARP.
			         1/2/Lt F.E. BRANDON. 1/2/Lt J.R. McDONALD
			
			O.C. "C" Coy. T/Capt. J. ROSS M.C. O.C. "D" Coy. 1/2/Lt. J.B. ALISON-HOPE.
			         2/Lt SWIRDWSELL 1/2 Lt R.M. MARTIN.
			         1/2/Lt J. CHERRY. 1/2 Lt W.J. FERNIE
			         2/Lt I. BENSON. 1/Lt J.R. McDONALD	

J Malley-Martin 2/Lt
B.I.O. 11th Border Regt.

WAR DIARY
or
INTELLIGENCE SUMMARY.

Army Form C. 2118.

11th Batt.
The Border Regt.

Place	Date	Hour	Summary of Events and Information	Remarks and references to Appendices
LINE S.W of -OMBARTZYDE	10-7-17	6.am	A heavy bombardment of our sector commenced about 6.a.m. The 1st & second lines were heavily "straffed" with "Minnenwerfers" also.	
		7.40am	The following message was sent to the 97th Inf. Bde at 7.40 am. "Begin" Casualties last night - 3 wounded men. This morning 1 killed man. Communication broken with both Coys in front line can when bombardment ceases will send further information "ends".	
		8.am	At 8.am the following message was received from O.C "C" Coy (Coy. holding 1st & 2nd line Right-half of Batt front. i.e. hose trench & its support). " I have been endeavouring to get a message through from here since 6.5.am. The wires are down & signallers are using the lamp but no reply from our artillery yet. We have been entirely "stafs" since before 6 am this morning with "heavin' etc. Please post punishment scheme & into operation at once". (Sd) J. Ross Capt. O.C "C" Coy 7.5.am ".	
		8.30am	Mr. Cook-Grey was sent by the C.O. to make his way to the front line Coys (C & D) in order to determine the exact state of affairs & the condition of the line. The shelling at this time was profusely getting heavier.	

J. Shaughrativ 1/L
M.I.O. XIIIth Border Regt

WAR DIARY
or
INTELLIGENCE SUMMARY.
(Erase heading not required.)

Army Form C. 2118.

11th Batt.
2. Border Regt.

Place	Date	Hour	Summary of Events and Information	Remarks and references to Appendices
LINE S.W. of LOMBARTZYDE	10-7-17	10 a.m.	At 10 a.m. the following message was received from 4/c Coot-Gray.— "I have reached and examined the second line. On the right the trench is somewhat dashed about but is not in really bad condition. There has been a continuous bombardment particularly with heavy T.M. 13" since 6 a.m. this morning." "5 casualties are reported at present. Our 18 M. shells are dropping short of don't think there is any dugout clear of that just this time." "10 a.m." "P.S." 18 M. have just smashed in a M.G.C. dugout in our second line." The bombardment increased in intensity about 10 a.m. All communication with Bde H.Q'rs was broken. 4/c CORE R.F.A. went out to O.P. K Sky and got thro' though but was unsuccessful.	JH
		10.40 a.m.	The following message was sent to "SOME" by pigeons (2) at 10.40 a.m. "Some 18ths pulling short in No 2 Battalion sector."	
		11-24 a.m.	Message received from Brigade. Report by runner situation whether first and support lines are intact and whether supporting companies are alright—also clear state of PUTNEY and VAUXHALL bridges. 11.24 a.m. End.	J Whalley-Kelly ?Lt n.98 2/Border Regt.

WAR DIARY
or
INTELLIGENCE SUMMARY.

Army Form C. 2118.

11th Batt.
The Border Regt.

Place	Date	Hour	Summary of Events and Information	Remarks and references to Appendices
LINE S.W. of LOMBARTZYDE.	10-7-17	11.24am	Following message received from Brigade at 11.24 am. Begin:- "1 Coy SPIN will reinforce No 1 Batt. 1 Coy SPUR will reinforce No 2 Batt. aaa SPOT & SPED will stiffen up third line NASM. Lieut aaa Coy SPIN & SPUR to move immediately upon receipt of these orders and come under orders of No 1 and 2 Batts. respectively. acknowledge." End.	
		11.50am	Following message sent to Brigade at 11.50 am. Begin:- "Cannot get any information as to 1st & 2nd line aaa They are being very heavily shelled aaa Hostile fire slackening aaa Will send off runners and report as soon as possible." End.	
		11.53am	Following message sent to A and B Coys (in support) Begin:- A and B Coy will be ready to turn out at a moment's notice - leading respective garrisons - Ammunition and give any information you have with estimated casualties." End. To O.C. No 1 & 2 Coys:- "Please state in writing (duplicate) condition of line and estimates of front line. Minenwerfer firing from M.22.B.55.40. Rgth predicts house on right of sector." End.	
		12.5pm	Following message recd from O.C. "A" Coy. Begin:- "Casualties til. Heavy T.M. Bombardment. Shelley Main 7/5 R.S.O. XI Border Regt.	

WAR DIARY or INTELLIGENCE SUMMARY

Army Form C. 2118.

11th Batt. The Border Regt.

Place	Date	Hour	Summary of Events and Information	Remarks and references to Appendices
LINE S.W of DMBARIZPDIE	10/7/17	12.25pm	Msg. recd from Brigade reads. "Keep your visual open to SHAG and the slightest sign of action on part of enemy infantry send S.O.S. and Brigade are out of touch with SHAG." End.	
		1.0pm	Following message sent to O.C. "B" Coy. "Following message sent to you at 11.53am is repeated. A & B Coys will be ready to turn out at a moments notice – Leaving respective garrisons. Acknowledge and give any information you have with estimated casualties." End. Please report thro' B.H.Q. at once and also send 3 men who knows the way to D Coy. Hqrs to BDE.B to act as runners." message end.	
		1.5pm	Enemy fire slackened a plane flew over very low (200ft) apparently to examine extent of damage. This machine was engaged by our M.G. teams gun. During this lull a new kind of gas shell was used causing every one to sneeze – it also affects the eyes, throat, skin some cases men followed by violent sickness.	
		1.25pm	Bombardment increased to original intensity.	
		1.45pm	Msg. recd. from Brigade. "A second company from SPIN ESPUR will reinforce htrs. 2 Battns respectively and Companies to come under order of hos. 1 & 2 Batta respectively, and Companies to move immediately." End.

J. Macey Martin /Lt
13 D.O. XI Border Regt

Army Form C. 2118.

WAR DIARY
or
INTELLIGENCE SUMMARY
(Erase heading not required.)

11th Batt.
The Border Regt.

Place	Date	Hour	Summary of Events and Information	Remarks and references to Appendices
LINE SW of BOMBARTZYDE	10/7/17	2.2/3.p.m	Following message rec'd by OC'A'Coy from 7/Lt SMYTHE whose rect with two platoons to reinforce 2nd line. "Arrived 3rd line 2-5 p.m – in comp'y 7/Li."	6
		2-3pm	hum rect from O.C. supporting Coy "A". "My two platoons have arrived at 3rd line at 2-5 p.m. Enemy barraging between 3rd & 2nd line with heavies." END.	
		2.30pm	Following message rec'd from OC'C'Coy. "The whole three lines are under a steady barrage. The lead-wires laid from my front line was satisfactory, but that is some time ago. At first had I.C. had endeavour to get news of that line. Owing to neither of either lamp signal in water. He looks grey with & after situation fully. My support and reserve platoons have had a rough passage but communication is impossible. Can you let me have any fresh orders or news." END.	
		"	Order of message rect from OC'A'Coy at 2-25pm sent to Brigade.	
		"	Message rec'd by OC'A'Coy from 7/Lt SMYTHE – "Second front-line heavily us about 15 us 2nd & 1st both are trenches to hold almost flat. Shall take company on to 2nd or stay in the 3rd line here. Perhaps hold in two places and & [pairs?] of sentries in No5 plat." end.	
		2-45pm	Message from OC. "Battle patrol must hold front-line whether cumulated or not." END.	

J. Macleymath. Lt.
R.D.C. 11th over reg. [?]

Army Form C. 2118.

WAR DIARY
or
INTELLIGENCE SUMMARY.
(Erase heading not required.)

11th Batt-
2/4 Border Regt.

Place	Date	Hour	Summary of Events and Information	Remarks and references to Appendices
LINE SW 1 LOMBARTZYDE	10/7/17	2.30p.	hrs sent to O.C. "C Coy" "Your note received. Patrols are to go forward to 2nd line and report and Brigade intends Battle patrols must hold front line whether demolished or not ans. Have you seen anything of "D Coy"? Ends.	
		3.0p.	2nd Coy 178 L.I. arrived to reinforce.	
		3.30p.	Lull in bombardment. Enemy future gun flew over very low & recognise for stretchers.	
		4-5pm.	Following message O.C. "C Coy" "Front-line very badly smashed now. Right half completely wiped out. Sentries very badly knocked about. from C H.Q. to N°15 Avenue non-existent. Third line receiving particular attention & badly knocked about. Comm trench heavy losses in stretchers ordered. Support casualties about 40. The shelling is very heavy throughout - continually on 1st 2nd & 3rd line comm trench. Have 2 officers in line now there exchanged with Rowies & sergt from 1st & 2nd line, when I have any myselves on the look out. My sergt Smith is also O.K. & have kept in touch with your O.P. Cook, Grey & 2/ my runners left in both O about 3pm. Schuill rly [railway] (as to get any news). We are lying low - hope service never stops it were much worn. I understand I am still here as the Company has just known up from here. Martin is slightly wounded." Ends	

Shirley Martin 2/Lt
R. D. O'Shea Border Regt

WAR DIARY
INTELLIGENCE SUMMARY.
(Erase heading not required.)

11th Batt.
The Border Regt.

Army Form C. 2118.

Place	Date	Hour	Summary of Events and Information	Remarks and references to Appendices
LINE SW of BOMBAFFE TYDE	16/7/17	4.40pm	Mr Cocker-Gray returns and gave a verbal account to the C.O.	
		5.0pm	2/Lt. Smythe reports – "He has only about 15 men left out of the two" "Platoons which went forward. During the lull an Enemy Aeroplane" "came over to observe. The 1st 2nd & 3rd lines are being very" "heavily shelled, especially the left of the 3rd. The fire in enfilade" "and there is very little shelter of any kind. He is keeping his men" "in 3rd line at present. The 1st & 2nd lines are perfectly flattened." "He does not think it advisable to send more men forward yet." Ends.	
		5.0pm	The following Message passed on from Lt. Rowell O.C. C Coy. – "I have about" "30 men left (including 1 of A Coy) all in left part of line. The other" "part very badly knocked about and untenable at present. It would" "be no use trying to send up any more before dusk. I have" "only the following N.C.Os. Sgt. Hill & L/Cpl Lyons. Both leave Guns." "(of 12+9) are out of action. Useless. It is impossible to try and" "recover casualties yet. Shall be glad when I can get facts out" "of this though I suppose you know we are in a hot place. Lt Cherry" "and servant arrived safely." Ends.	

WAR DIARY
or
INTELLIGENCE SUMMARY

Army Form C. 2118.

11th Batt. The Border Regt

Place	Date	Hour	Summary of Events and Information	Remarks and references to Appendices
Line SW of Lombard-zyde	10/7/17	5.5 pm	The following Message sent to O.C. "B" Coy:— "Mr Smythes report re "I cannot understand" "Lines not at all bad one. Other report says first and second" "Lines from Third?" Ends "Can he are condition of 1st & 2nd"	
		5.20 pm	Following Message received from O.C. "B" Coy:— "This is the statement "of the Patrols. He can see the 1st & 2nd Lines they look very much" "flattened"	
		5.50 pm	Fell in Shelling. Gas shells being used again. Enemy Plane flying low over lines.	
		5.25 pm	Shelling increased to original intensity	
		5.30 pm	Following Message received from O.C. "B" Coy:— "Mr Smythe sends "word that he has only four men left. Can I send another" "Platoon to him?"	
		6.30 pm	Following Message sent to C & D Coys:— "Your notes received re "Your munitions are to hold on & Front line at all costs are Posts" "are to be established in front line as soon as possible as Reinforcement" "are being sent up gradually to both Coys by tracks are All dsunal." "Messages are to be sent & times and repeats from both Coys if possible as" "5 pm." Ends. H. Rosehaft	

Smalldetachment Mr Cook-Gray arrived safely about 5 pm. H. Rosehaft

Army Form C. 2118.

11th Batt
The Border Regt

10

WAR DIARY
or
INTELLIGENCE SUMMARY.
(Erase heading not required.)

Instructions regarding War Diaries and Intelligence Summaries are contained in F. S. Regs., Part II. and the Staff Manual respectively. Title pages will be prepared in manuscript.

Place	Date	Hour	Summary of Events and Information	Remarks and references to Appendices
We Sh of Tortarel Gybe	10/11/17	6.50 pm	Following Message sent to O.C. B.Coy. "Have your boy ready" "to move and Report here at once". Ends.	
		7.30 pm	Following Message received from O.C. C.Coy. "Enemy held Nose Trench" "I am still in Nose support but have only five men 4 Lt. Ridgway" "Send reinforcements. Am in trench at my Coy H.Q." Ends. Shelling slackened considerably. Enemy Plane over Grand Reden flying very low. 500 ft. Enemy reported as having gained a footing in 2nd line and part of 3rd.	
		7.50 pm	2nd Coys 17th H.L.I. were ordered to counter attack immediately. All Garrison of the Reden standing to. Every available Rifle being used to defend Grand and Petit Reden	
		7.50 pm	Following Message sent to O.C. A.Coy. "Have your boy ready to" "move and Report here at once". Ends.	
		7.55 pm	Following Message sent to Brigade "Left Coy Commander reports:-" "Enemy in Nose Trench ___ Have ordered 2 Coys H.L.I. to counter" "attack ___ Garrison of Reden and Huitrieres are standing to". Ends.	J. Hougach Lt Col D.O. XI Border Regt

WAR DIARY
INTELLIGENCE SUMMARY.

Army Form C. 2118.

1st Batt.
The Border Regt.

Place	Date	Hour	Summary of Events and Information	Remarks and references to Appendices
Line SW of Lombard-Syke	16/11/17	7.50 pm	Roughly estimate casualties and condition of your front line troops and Do you want one more Coy sent up as the bearer of this will bring back reply.	
		7.56 pm	Send three more orderlies to Brigade H.Q.	
		8.0 pm	Message sent to A & B Coys:- "Stand to garrison of Redan and Huitrieres. Enemy in Nose Trench." Ends.	
		8.3 pm	Message sent from Brig. H.Q. " One Company SPOR will report to SPED immediately on receipt of this order and they will come under orders of SPED and Acknowledge" Ends.	
		8.15 pm	Message sent from Brig. H.Q.:- "Enemy patrols reported on left front line an line must be established at once and every effort made to send patrols of real troops over to enemy line and Acknowledge." Ends.	
		8.40 pm	Message sent from B.H.Q.:- "One Company SPIN will report to SPED immediately on receipt of this and acknowledge" Ends.	
		9.5 pm	Message sent from Lt Malby Martin:- " H.L.I. have received orders to withdraw from G. Redan. I have conformed with them and await orders." Ends.	
		9.20 pm	Message sent to B.H.Q. "Two Companies H.L.I. under Capt. Stevens have advanced from Grand Redan to Hit Line where they will"	

WAR DIARY
or
INTELLIGENCE SUMMARY

Army Form C. 2118.

1st Batt:
The Border Regt.

Place	Date	Hour	Summary of Events and Information	Remarks and references to Appendices
Nieuport Sw. of La Fatigue	10/7/17	9.20 pm	Message Continued "Dig in and remain until further reinforcements as in your "B.M. 205 am I have two – all Battn. H.Q. servants re-holding Grand "Redan as Detached party have moved along bank of Rooms to "Huthwaite to protect left flank and when reinforcements H.L.I. "will advance to 3rd line and further if situation permits" Ends.	
		9.25 pm	Message sent to 2/Lt Mackay Martin:– "No one retired from Grand "Redan until definite orders have been received from N/Col Girdwood "Get everybody into Grand Redan and stay there" Ends.	
		9.30 pm	Message sent to BHQ :– "Capt. Ross XI 10th Borders reports that 16th H.L.I. "have retired beyond 3rd line and Sergt. McShank reports that the "Right Battn of 1st Division wiped out and another Battn has "retired and I do not feel justified in advancing beyond 3rd line "with flanks unprotected an advance will commence as soon as "our Coy SPUR and one Coy SPIN arrive as not yet reported to me are "two Platoons at Huthwaite reported still intact. Can you inform me "if 16th H.L.I. and 1st Division are also going to advance. Also when" Ends.	

Smallthwaite Lt.-Col.
C.O. XI Border Regt.

WAR DIARY or INTELLIGENCE SUMMARY

Army Form C. 2118.

11th Battn. The Border Regt.

Place	Date	Hour	Summary of Events and Information	Remarks and references to Appendices
Line S.W. of Embanksyde	18/11/17	10.5 pm	Message received from 2/Lt Mallay Martin:— "Am on left of Grand Redan" "On top. Holding. M.G. have a gun in Nose" Ends.	
		10.20 pm	Message received from Capt Stevens 17th H.L.I. "SPOT report holding support line and patrols sent forward to re-establish posts in front line an SPAR" Ends	
		10.20 pm	Message sent to Capt Stevens 17th H.L.I. "Your 3rd Coy has come up and will report to you with this letter. Push forward fighting patrols at once to 3rd line, and as soon as they are established dribble men forward and form posts to cover our decisive limit. Nose Avenue to Nose Lane." "The 3rd Coy will remain in 4th line till you are established in 3rd line" "Then you will bring up the 3rd Coy and push one patrol to 2nd line" "and finally to 1st line if possible." "Your 3rd Coy are all keen to be helped by small posts which must be dug in at once an reserve are all keen to be held by small posts which tonight as you will probably be there all tomorrow. Dig hard and don't move about in daylight. Report situation as often as possible. Acknowledge" Ends	
		10.25 pm	Message sent to Lt Smyth:— "Lt Smyth will be in command of all troops in Grand Redan. No one to leave G. Redan without definite order in"	J. Hutton 4/5 B.O. Border Regt

J. Hutton
B.O. Border Regt.

WAR DIARY
or
INTELLIGENCE SUMMARY.

Army Form C. 2118.

11th Batt.
The Border Regt.

Place	Date	Hour	Summary of Events and Information	Remarks and references to Appendices
See Sn of 16/7 Embarkydn	14/7/17	10.25pm	Message cont'd "Waiting from me except to make report at H.Q. Inform all officers." Ends.	
		10.50pm	Message sent to Lt Smythe :- "You are to descending up very "fight". 17th H.L.I. now in H.Q. line are about to advance are 16th H.L.I." "Have reached Support Trench. Send Malloy Martin back to Batt: H.Q." Ends	
		11.20pm	Message sent to Capt. Stevens :- "Your 3rd Coy instead of following" "you will move along 4th line to Nose Lane where they will form a " "defensive flank " to your left as you advance. The 16th H.L.I. have" "reached 2nd line are advance as quickly as possible. Acknowledge." Ends	
		11.45pm	Message sent to B.H.Q. :- "3 Coy H.L.I. now in position and K.O.Y.L.I. Coy" "not yet arrived." Ends.	
	11/1/17	12.15am	Message sent from Capt Greenhill O.C. No.1 Coy :- "The position at the" "Multiture is that the defences have been blown in. My platoons are" "in Nose Lane and in touch with the SPUR. Casualties 4." Ends.	
		12.25am	Message sent to O.C. C Coy H.L.I. :- "You are to report at once with your Coy" "to Capt Stevens in H.Q. line and 2/Lt Book Gray bearer of this will guide" "you to the Head Quarters and you will act under his orders." Ends. Whitley Mart 2/Lt A.D.O. XI Border Regt.	Whitley

WAR DIARY or INTELLIGENCE SUMMARY

Army Form C. 2118.

11th Batt.
Th. Border Regt.

Place	Date	Hour	Summary of Events and Information	Remarks and references to Appendices
Line S.W. of Lembartzyde	11/7/17	12.30am	Message sent from B.H.Q. to O.C. 2"g M.G.C :- "Your Guns will proceed to" "Respirle to cover the left flanks of the 11th Borders an Your Guns will" "report to O.C. 11th Borders to cover the left flank as 11th Borders H.Q." "are at the Powder Magazine. Address my M.G. Coy repeats Div. M.G.O" "11th Borders"	
		12.45am	Message received by O.C. Coy. 2" Vigili. "6 Coy 2nd K.O.Y.L.I will move" from 11th Borders H.Q. to the place where it will report to Capt. Stevens" "Commanding B. Coy 17th H.L.I. His H.Q. are in 4th Line between Nose Alley" "and Nose Lane as they will act under his orders." Ends	
		12.45am	Message sent from B.H.Q. :- "As soon as the 11th Borders have re-established" "a line they will be relieved by the 16th Northumberland Fusiliers and Colonel" "Scully will proceed to H.Q. 11th Borders and arrange all details of relief" "direct with them as Relief to be completed before Daylight and 2 i/c" "Nieuport defences at present held by the 16th N.F. will be taken over by" "the 15th Lancashire Fus - all details to be arranged between Commanding" "officers concerned. The 15th Lancs Fus. will take over the same dispositions" "as the 16th North. Fusiliers." Ends	
		12.45am	Message received by Capt. Stevens 17th H.L.I. "2nd Platoons S.P.E.D. are in Nose" "Lane having been obliged to evacuate the Huitrieres owing to Shelling. They are"	

J Watts
Lt. Col.
11th Border Regt.

WAR DIARY or INTELLIGENCE SUMMARY

Army Form C. 2118

1st Batt.
The Border Regt.

16

Place	Date	Hour	Summary of Events and Information	Remarks and references to Appendices
Trenches S.W. of Combles	11/11/17	1.45 am	Message Cont:d "to be in touch with your left and Report the situation by the runner and push forward as rapidly as possible to get in line with 16th H.L.I." Endo.	
		1.20 am	Message sent from Capt Stevens 17th H.L.I:- "Patrol met SPED Officer in 3rd line who says 1st 2nd & 3rd lines are held by SPED. Am sending up 3 Platoons (on Regt of Noes Alley) I have not heard about the left as yet." Endo	
		1.20 am	Message received by Lt Smythe. "You are to order all the men of Batt: H.Qrs to return to Bde HQrs and take up their original dug outs." Endo	
		1.45 am	Message sent by Lt Martin. O.C. B Coy & B Coy SORP " B. Coy SPUR in position in 4th." Endo	
		1.45 am	Message received by O.C. A+B Coys. "11th Border Regt. is to be relieved tonight by 16th N. Fus:rs A+B Coys will each send 4 Guides to Battn "H Qts immediately on receipt of this order. Guides will be able to "guide relieving Coys to 3rd line – A. Coy to Right subsector & B Coy to left "subsector an on completion of Relief A+B Coys will each withdraw "to Grand Redan and Accommodation must be found there for all details "a further orders." Endo.	J Mills Junk Lt 1/15 R.D.O. 1 Border Regt –

WAR DIARY
or
INTELLIGENCE SUMMARY

Army Form C. 2118

1st Batt.
The Border Regt.

Place	Date	Hour	Summary of Events and Information	Remarks and references to Appendices
Trenches S. W. of Nieuport embarking by the 11th Border Regt.	11/7/17	12.15 am.	Message sent from B.H.Q. "As soon as the 11th Borders are established and are they will be relieved by the 10th"	
		1.45 am.	Message sent by Lt Macfarlane:— "We are holding our sector completely intact and have 3 Patrols out in No Man's Land and no attempt has been made by the enemy to penetrate our lines." Ends.	
		2. am	Message sent from B.H.Q.:— "You must work at once to your left and help the 11th Border. Addressed 16th H.L.I. repeated 11th Border." Ends.	
		2. am	Message sent from Capt. Stevens 17th H.L.I.:— "I am sending up another patrol. Platoons to 3rd line to right of Nose Alley. They have at present a patrol out to 2nd line. On the left I am told the 3rd line is empty 'absolutely flat' & a Patrol up Nose Lane has not come back though it has been out 2 hours. I am sending up 2 Platoons into the 3rd line on left with strong flank guard. Am going to put 3 strong posts in the Lane with a patrol out while it is dark." Ends.	
		2.25 am.	Message sent from B.H.Q.:— "On relief the 11th Borders will return to 'Newarrade' ard the 3 Companies 17th H.L.I. and one Company K.O.Y.L.I. at present attached to 11th Borders will be attached to 16th Northumberland Fus. and come under the orders of O.C. North. Fus. on completion of relief." Ends.	

J. Mealeyhall 1/7 R.D.O. 1st Border Regt.

WAR DIARY or INTELLIGENCE SUMMARY

Army Form C. 2118

11th Batt. The Border Regt.

Place	Date	Hour	Summary of Events and Information	Remarks and references to Appendices
Erie Sap Embankment	11/7/17	2.30 am	Message received by Capt. Stevens. O.C. 17th H.L.I:- "You must push on quickly" "to 2nd line where you will get in touch with 16th H.L.I. and there you will" "establish Posts and send forward patrols to 1st line which should also" "be occupied. 16th H.L.I. are in their 1st line with Patrols in No Man's Land." "You will be relieved probably by 16th North'd Fusiliers who will come up" "when you are established in 2nd line. Move rapidly forward" Ends.	
		2.45 am	Message sent by B.H.Q'rs:- "17th H.L.I. holding Bosquile defences will pay" "particular attention to its left in New Trench near its junction with" "1st line: an Enemy is reported to be attempting to hedge in this locality." Ends.	
		3.30 am	Message sent to B.H.Q'rs by R. Hodgkinson:- "Estimated Casualties" "Today (10/11/17) S.P.E.D. 1 Capt. 7 Subalterns. 350 other Ranks."	
		4. am	Message received by O.C. A & B. Coys:- A & B. Coys will withdraw to "support dug-outs immediately on receipt of this order. 'A' Coy" "to position in New Wood. 'B' Coy to position recently occupied by" "'C' Coy" Ends.	

J Molyneux —?/Lt
B.H.Q. XI Border Regt.

INTELLIGENCE SUMMARY.
(Erase heading not required.)

1st Border Regt.

19

Place	Date	Hour	Summary of Events and Information	Remarks and references to Appendices
NIEUPORT	11/7/17	10 pm	Batt. was relieved by 16th D.L.I by 4.30 am. marched to new Parade.	
COXYDE	12/7/17	"	Batt. arrived at COXYDE at 5.30 am. Day spent in rest.	
"	13/7/17	"	Rest in rest. Evening lit alarm lit at 10.30 pm	
"	14/7/17	"	" "	
"	15/7/17	"	Batt. church parade 10 am.	
GHYVELDE	16/7/17	"	Batt. left COXYDE at 5.30 am and marched to GHYVELDE via LA PANNE – ADINKERKE. Arrived 8.30 am.	
"	17/7/17	"	Batn. training in dunes until 1.45 pm.	
"	18/7/17	"	" " " " " alw practising attack on embarkation arches	
"	19/7/17	"	" " " "	
BRAY-DUNES	20/7/17	"	Batt. left GHYVELDE at 5.30 am marched to camp in BRAY DUNES. Sea Bathing & recreation.	
"	21/7/17	"	training & recreation.	

J. Moseyhurst Lt
R.S.M. 1st Border Regt

WAR DIARY
or
INTELLIGENCE SUMMARY.
(Erase heading not required.)

Army Form C. 2118.

11th Batta the Border Regt

No. 20

Place	Date	Hour	Summary of Events and Information	Remarks and references to Appendices
S RAY-DU MONT	22/7/17	10 a.m.	Church parade 10 a.m. Recreation - bathing & men etc.	
"	23/7/17	"	Working parties.	
"	24/7/17	"	Practice attack on strong point with live ammunition. Demolition of M M G Corp Club.	
"	25/7/17	"	Working parties laying pipe line during day.	
COXYDE	26/7/17	"	Batt. moved to COXYDE at 6.45 am arriving at 9.30 am. Two Coys on working party.	
"	27/7/17	"	Two Coys on working party - digging cable trenches. Back round to Camp from BATT. at 3.30 pm.	
"	28/7/17	"	1 Coy on working party - 1 Coy on night-working party. Two Coys on night-working party.	
"	29/7/17	"	Coys on working parties during day & night.	
"	30/7/17	"	Batt. ordered to move to La PANNE at 2-p.m which was count. order. Move cancelled at 1.45 pm.	
"	31/7/17	"	Batt. training specials during day. Inspection etc.	

Hanwey hush to
R.S.O. ℅ Border Regt:

J.E. Cor Hun M/m
Comdg. 11 Border Regt

CONFIDENTIAL.

War Diary
of
11th Border Regiment
From 1st August to 31st August
(Volume No. 21.)

Army Form C. 2118.

WAR DIARY
or
INTELLIGENCE SUMMARY.

(Erase heading not required.)

11th Battalion,
The Border Regiment.

Instructions regarding War Diaries and Intelligence Summaries are contained in F. S. Regs., Part II. and the Staff Manual respectively. Title pages will be prepared in manuscript.

Place	Date	Hour	Summary of Events and Information	Remarks and references to Appendices
COXYDE	WED 1-8-14	10 am	Work impossible owing to heavy rain all day. Capt. Anderson - Regtl. Medical Officer in orders for the P.S.O. for his work on July 9th-10th M.M. Sh booking for M.C. on same date. JCB.	
"	THUR 2-8-14	10 am	Heavy rain continues. Outdoor work impossible. Indoor training carried on. JCB	
"	FRI 3-8-14	"	Heavy rain still continues. Indoor work and Lectures carried on. JCB.	
"	4-8-14	"	Rain during morning. Training in Recreation. JCB	
"	5-8-14	"	Training under Company arrangements JCB	
"	6-8-14	"	" " " Sea bathing in the afternoon JCB	
"	7-8-14	"	" " " " " JCB.	
"	8-8-14	"	" " " JCB	
"	9-8-14	"	" " " JCB	
"	10-8-14	"	Batt moved to OOST-DUNKERQUE at 10 am. JCB	
"	11-8-14	"	Training carried out under Coy arrangements JCB	
"	12-8-14	"	Church parade at 10 am JCB.	
"	13-8-14	"	Cleaning up billets. Inspection by D.A.D.M.S. JCB.	

Army Form C. 2118.

WAR DIARY
or
INTELLIGENCE SUMMARY.

(Erase heading not required.)

1th Battn
The Border Regt.

Instructions regarding War Diaries and Intelligence
Summaries are contained in F. S. Regs., Part II.
and the Staff Manual respectively. Title pages
will be prepared in manuscript.

Place	Date	Hour	Summary of Events and Information	Remarks and references to Appendices
DUNKERQUE	14-8-17	10 p.m.	Battn marched to BRAY-DUNES at 9.30 a.m. arriving at 1 p.m. JLB. Training under Coy arrangements. Sea Bathing in afternoon JLB.	
BRAY-DUNES	15-8-17	"	"	JLB
	16-8-17	"	"	JLB
	17-8-17	"	Battn moved to GHYVELDE at 9 a.m. Battn church parade at 10 a.m. Recreation etc. JLB.	
	18-8-17	"		JLB
	19-8-17	"		
	20-8-17	"	Battn training in Div Attack & rapid consolidation etc. JLB.	
	21-8-17	"	Battn went to BRAY DUNES at 9 a.m. for Range Practice and Bathing returning to billets in GHYVELDE at 6 p.m. JLB.	
	22-8-17	"	Battn training in 32nd Divisional Attack Scheme in the morning. Shorts training in the afternoon. JLB.	
	23-8-17	"	A & C Coys practised Rapid Consolidation, B & D Musketry and firing. Afternoon sports JLB. B & C " " "	JLB
	24-8-17	"	94th Brigade sports — no parades. JLB.	
	25-8-17	"	Battn bathed at Divisional Baths PONT DE GHYVELDE. Major J. F. Tweed took over command JLB	
	26-8-17	"	Battn moved at 1.30 p.m. to CANADA CAMP via BRAY DUNES along the beach past LA PANNE JLB	

WAR DIARY
or
INTELLIGENCE SUMMARY.

Army Form C. 2118.

Place	Date	Hour	Summary of Events and Information	Remarks and references to Appendices
CANADA CAMP	28-8-19	10 p.m.	to ST IDESBALDE thence inland to CANADA CAMP arriving 6.30 p.m. JFT	
OST DUNKERQUE	29-8-19	"	Battn moved to OOST DUNKERQUE as Divisional Reserve at 8.50 p.m. arriving 9.50 p.m. JFT	
"	30-8-19	"	Rain during morning. Cleaning up billets. JFT	
"	31-8-19	"	Training under Coy arrangements. Working parties at night. JFT	

J F Tweed Major,
Commanding, 11th Border Regiment.

Confidential.

War Diary
of
11th Border Regiment.
From 1st September 1917 to 30th September 1917
(Volume 22).

Army Form C. 2118.

WAR DIARY
or
INTELLIGENCE SUMMARY.
(Erase heading not required.)

Instructions regarding War Diaries and Intelligence Summaries are contained in F. S. Regs., Part II. and the Staff Manual respectively. Title pages will be prepared in manuscript.

Place	Date	Hour	Summary of Events and Information	Remarks and references to Appendices

2353 Wt. W2544/1454 7co,ooo 5/15 D. D. & L. A.D.S.S./Form, C. 2118.

Army Form C. 2118.

WAR DIARY
or
INTELLIGENCE SUMMARY.
(Erase heading not required.)

XI Corps

Vol 22

Place	Date	Hour	Summary of Events and Information	Remarks and references to Appendices
Post-Dunkerque	1/9/17		The Village was shelled considerably with long distance high velocity guns and during the night. 31st July. Transport Lines were hit and 4 Officers Chargers killed.	
do	2/9/17		Batt. finding Working Parties. Operation Orders received from Brigade.	
do	3/9/17		Batt. relieved 19th A.C.I. in the Left Sub-Sector St. Georges Sector. the first Company marched off at 8.30 p.m. Relief was complete at midnight. Disposition of Batt. as follows. A Coy on the right, B Coy on the left, C Coy in Support, garrisoning 2 farms on the Polders, D Coy in Brigade Reserve, acting as carrying parties for the front line Coys.	
In the Line	4/9/17		Front comparatively quiet. Trenches consist of breast work only not in a very good state of repair. There is an absolute break between the Left Coy Front and Right Coy Front, caused by a bridge over a large dyke being broken down. 7 men wounded.	
do	5/9/17		Comparatively quiet. Slight shelling on Left Coy Front 1 man killed 2 men wounded.	

Army Form C. 2118.

WAR DIARY
or
INTELLIGENCE SUMMARY.
(Erase heading not required.)

Instructions regarding War Diaries and Intelligence Summaries are contained in F. S. Regs., Part II. and the Staff Manual respectively. Title pages will be prepared in manuscript.

Place	Date	Hour	Summary of Events and Information	Remarks and references to Appendices
In the Line	6/9/17		Some "Minnies' troublesome on Left Coy front. 2/Lt. A. Turner killed & 3 O.R. wounded.	244A
do	7/9/17		Fairly quiet. Gas put over on the front. Enemy made practically no retaliation. 2 O.R. wounded	244A
do	8/9/17		Some Shelling on the Bricksocks and Left Coy front. 2 O.R. killed. 3 O.R. wounded. Operation Orders received from Brigade.	244A 244B
do	9/9/17		Quiet. 1 man wounded.	244B
do	10/9/17		Early in the morning the Battn. was relieved on the line by the 2nd K.O.Y.L.I. and proceeded to Billets in WULPEN. Relief quiet.	244A
WULPEN	11/9/17		No one allowed on streets during day, owing to enemy Balloon observation. Time spent in cleaning billets and working parties by night.	244A 244A
do	12/9/17		Everything quiet.	244A
do	13/9/17		Battn. finding working parties.	244A
do	14/9/17		do	244A
do	15/9/17		Battn. relieved 19th K.L.I. on the Right Sub Sector, St. Georges Sector, first Coy marching off at 8 p.m. Relief quiet and complete at 11-30 p.m. Disposition of	

WAR DIARY
or
INTELLIGENCE SUMMARY.

(Erase heading not required.)

Army Form C. 2118.

Place	Date	Hour	Summary of Events and Information	Remarks and references to Appendices
In the line	16/9/17		Battⁿ. as follows: C Coy on the right, D Coy on the left, A Coy in support at WHITE HOUSE & B Coy in Reserve at GROOTE LABEUR FARM. B.H.Q. VACHE GRVEE. Went quiet.	Appx 28
do	17/9/17		Raid on C Coy lines about 3-30 a.m. Loss 1 OR killed and 1 O.R. wounded. Heavy hostile bombardment on left sub-sector (ST GEORGES and LOMBARTZYDE) During afternoon a Bosche wounded during raid on C Company was brought into our lines.	Appx
do	18/9/17		Germans used megaphone from ALPHA POST to C Coy POST.	Appx
do	19/9/17		German came out of ALPHA POST towards C Coy POST. Later 2/Lt. N.Y. Ridgway went out from C Coy Post to meet German who came out of ALPHA Post.	Appx
do	20/9/17		There was no result from these advances. Question Ordrs received from Brigade British Aeroplane down at KETTLERDAM BRIDGE. Pilot rescued. Relieved by 15th H.L.I. and went into billets at COXYDE.	Appx

WAR DIARY
or
INTELLIGENCE SUMMARY.
(Erase heading not required.)

Army Form C. 2118.

Place	Date	Hour	Summary of Events and Information	Remarks and references to Appendices
COXYDE	21/9/17		Left COXYDE at 2pm and marched to LAPANNE in Divisional Reserve. Operation Orders received from Bgde	YA/18
LA PANNE	22/9/17		Left LA PANNE by sea route for ZUYDCOOTE and took over from 1st K.O.Y.L.I.	YA/43
ZUYDCOOTE	23/9/17		Church Parade. Operation Orders received from Brigade.	YA/44
do	24/9/17		Marched from ZUYDCOOTE to LA PANNE by Sea Route	YA/45
LA PANNE	25/9/17		Battn finding working parties	YA/46
do	26/9/17		" " " " Lecture to all Officers & Platoon Sgts by Divisional Commander. 16 OR proceeding on wiring attachment	YA/46
do	27/9/17		Battn finding Working parties. Very practicing Aheen fence wiring. Operation Orders received from Bgde	YA/47
do	28/9/17		Battn relieved 13th Lancashire Fusiliers in LEFFRINCKOUCKE Battn in the LOMBARTZYDE Sector, with B.H.Q. in "Ruffey House". Transport employed by Div. Com.	YA/48
In the Line	29/9/17		Battn finding Working Parties from front line Battalion. B Coy carrying party led astray by R.E. guide, which resulted in 1 OR being wounded & missing and 1 OR wounded (SS). 1 OR killed at B.H.Q. 2/Lt D. Walker and 3 OR wounded.	YA/6
do	30/9/17		Battn finding Working parties. 1 OR Died of Wounds. 2 OR killed 1 OR killed & 3 OR wounded.	YA/6 YA/6

M.H. Hopkinson Capt
2 Border Regt.

CONFIDENTIAL

War Diary
of
11th Border Regiment
1st to 31st October 1917.
(Volume. No 23)

Army Form C. 2118.

WAR DIARY
or
INTELLIGENCE SUMMARY.

(Erase heading not required.)

Instructions regarding War Diaries and Intelligence Summaries are contained in F. S. Regs., Part II. and the Staff Manual respectively. Title pages will be prepared in manuscript.

Place	Date	Hour	Summary of Events and Information	Remarks and references to Appendices

Army Form C. 2118.

WAR DIARY
or
INTELLIGENCE SUMMARY.
(Erase heading not required.)

Place	Date	Hour	Summary of Events and Information	Remarks and references to Appendices
the Line	1/10/19		Battalion held left subsector of BOMBARDZYDE SECTOR. Dispositions unchanged. 5/R. S.G.M.have wounded 5 other ranks killed, 5 other ranks wounded	h. S.
the Line	2/10/19		Dispositions unchanged. 14 other ranks wounded, 1 other rank killed	h. S.
the Line	3/10/19		Dispositions unchanged. 2 other ranks killed 8 other ranks wounded	h. S.
the Line	4/10/19		Dispositions unchanged 1 other rank wounded	h. S.
the Line	5/10/19		4 other ranks wounded. Battalion relieved by 10th Batt Lancashire Fusiliers, and withdrew to CANADA CAMP, relief quiet and completed at 11.30pm.	h. S.
COXYDE	6/10/19		Battalion marched to ADINKERKE, and proceeded to ROSENDAEL by Barge, thence by march route to TETEGHEM, arriving about 8pm.	h. S.
TETEGHEM	7/10/19		Time devoted to cleaning of equipment etc., and improving of billets	h. S.
do	8/10/19		Selection of training grounds for companies. Recreation in the afternoon.	

Army Form C. 2118.

WAR DIARY
or
INTELLIGENCE SUMMARY.
(Erase heading not required.)

Instructions regarding War Diaries and Intelligence Summaries are contained in F. S. Regs., Part II. and the Staff Manual respectively. Title pages will be prepared in manuscript.

Place	Date	Hour	Summary of Events and Information	Remarks and references to Appendices
TETEGHEM	9/10/19		Coys at disposal of Coy Commanders for training. Specialist training carried out. Recreation in the afternoon.	n. S.
TETEGHEM	10/10/19		Coys at disposal of Coy Commanders for Physical Drill, & Rifle firing practice during morning, and Specialist training carried out. Recreation in the afternoon.	n. S.
do	11/10/19		Coys practicing Platoons in the Attack. Recreation in the afternoon	n. S.
do	12/10/19		" " " " " " and deploying for the attack.	n. S.
do	13/10/19		Coys at disposal of Coy Commanders. Specialist training carried out. Recreation in the afternoon.	n. S.
do	14/10/19		Church parade at 10 am for A & C Coys and for B & D Coys at 11 am.	n. S.
do	15/10/19		A, B, & D Coys at disposal of Coy Commanders for Physical Drill & musketry during morning. C Coy on 6 miles route march. Recreation in the afternoon.	n. S.
do	16/10/19		A, C, & D Coys at disposal of Coy Commanders for Physical Drill & musketry during morning. B Coy on 6 miles route march. Recreation in the afternoon.	n. S.

WAR DIARY
or
INTELLIGENCE SUMMARY.
(Erase heading not required)

Army Form C. 2118.

Instructions regarding War Diaries and Intelligence Summaries are contained in F. S. Regs., Part II. and the Staff Manual respectively. Title pages will be prepared in manuscript.

Place	Date	Hour	Summary of Events and Information	Remarks and references to Appendices
TETEGHEM	17/10/14		B, C, & D Coys at disposal of Coy Commanders for Physical Drills & Musketry during morning. Coys on 6 miles route march. Recreation in the afternoon	M.S.
do	18/10/14		Battalion marched to FORT-DES-DUNES and carried out practice attack. returning to billets at 3 p.m.	M.S.
do	19/10/14		Coys carried out 6 mile route march in full marching order, and 2 hours Coy training during morning. Recreation in the afternoon	M.S.
do	20/10/14		Battalion marched to FORT-DES-DUNES and carried out practice attack. Specialists on specialist training. Football competition during afternoon	M.S.
do	21/10/14		Battalion Church Parade at 10.30 a.m.	M.S.
do	22/10/14		Coys & H.Q. carried out 6 miles route march independantly in full marching Order commencing at 9 a.m.	M.S.
do	23/10/14		Coys at disposal of Coy Commanders for training. Recreation in the afternoon	M.S.
do	24/10/14		Battalion marched off at 8.15 a.m. to ZEGERS CAPPEL arriving at 1 p.m.	M.S.
ZEGERS CAPPEL	25/10/14		Battalion marched off at 11.15 a.m. to ROUBROUCK Area arriving in billets at 1 p.m.	M.S.

Place	Date	Hour	Summary of Events and Information	Remarks and references to Appendices
ROUBROUCK AREA	26/10/17		Coys at the disposal of Coy Commanders for cleaning up and indoor work. Specialists carried out specialist training.	h.S.
ROUBROUCK AREA	29/10/17		7. to 00 Lectures during morning. Stretcher Bearers under Medical Officer from 10 to 12 am & from 2 to 4 pm. Battalion carried out attack practice during afternoon	h.S.
ROUBROUCK AREA	28/10/17		Battalion carried out practice attack at dawn, zero hour 5.30 a.m.	h.S.
ROUBROUCK AREA	29/10/17		Church parades held for Coys	h.S.
ROUBROUCK AREA	30/10/17		Coys at disposal of Coy Commanders. Coy training	h.S.
ROUBROUCK AREA	31/10/17		Coy training	h.S.

CONFIDENTIAL

War Diary
of
11th Border Regiment
From 1st to 30th November, 1914
(Volume No. 24)

Vol 24

Army Form C. 2118.

WAR DIARY
or
INTELLIGENCE SUMMARY.

(Erase heading not required.)

Instructions regarding War Diaries and Intelligence Summaries are contained in F. S. Regs., Part II. and the Staff Manual respectively. Title pages will be prepared in manuscript.

Place	Date	Hour	Summary of Events and Information	Remarks and references to Appendices

(A7592). Wt. W12896/M1293. 75 500. 1/17. D. D. & L., Ltd. Forms/C.2118/14.

Army Form C. 2118.

WAR DIARY
or
INTELLIGENCE SUMMARY.
(Erase heading not required.)

Instructions regarding War Diaries and Intelligence Summaries are contained in F. S. Regs., Part II. and the Staff Manual respectively. Title pages will be prepared in manuscript.

Place	Date	Hour	Summary of Events and Information	Remarks and references to Appendices
UBROUCK AREA	1/11/17		Coys at the disposal of Coy Commanders for training	h.S.
UBROUCK AREA	2/11/17		Coys at the disposal of Coy Commanders for training.	h.S.
UBROUCK AREA	3/11/17		Church parade. Memorial Service to the late Chaplain Langston P.F. at 2.0 pm	h.S.
UBROUCK AREA	4/11/17		Battalion training.	h.S.
UBROUCK AREA	5/11/17		Battalion training.	h.S.
UBROUCK AREA	6/11/17		Battalion training.	h.S.
UBROUCK AREA	7/11/17		Battalion training	h.S.
UBROUCK AREA	8/11/17		Battalion inspected by the Cof S Brown Divisional Commander at 11 am	h.S.
UBROUCK AREA	9/11/17		Battalion training. Operation order received	h.S.
UBROUCK AREA	10/11/17		Battalion marched to the WINNEZEELE AREA at 7.10 am arrived 12.0 hrs.	h.S.
WINNEZEELE AREA	11/11/17		Battalion marched to ROAD CAMP at 8.18 am arrived 12.0 hrs.	h.S.
ROAD CAMP	12/11/17		Inspections and general cleaning up of camp.	h.S.
ROAD CAMP	13/11/17		Battalion training.	h.S.
ROAD CAMP	14/11/17		Battalion training.	h.S.

WAR DIARY
or
INTELLIGENCE SUMMARY.
(Erase heading not required.)

Army Form C. 2118.

Instructions regarding War Diaries and Intelligence Summaries are contained in F. S. Regs., Part II. and the Staff Manual respectively. Title pages will be prepared in manuscript.

Place	Date	Hour	Summary of Events and Information	Remarks and references to Appendices
ROAD CAMP	15/11/17		Battalion Training. Divisional Commander inspected the Camp.	h.S.
ROAD CAMP	16/11/17		Battalion Training. Corps Commander inspected the Camp.	h.S.
ROAD CAMP	17/11/17		Battalion improving camp.	h.S.
ROAD CAMP	18/11/17		Battalion training.	h.S.
ROAD CAMP	19/11/17		Battalion Training.	h.S.
ROAD CAMP	20/11/17		Battalion training.	h.S.
ROAD CAMP	21/11/17		Battalion training.	h.S.
HILL TOP FARM	22/11/17		Battalion left ROAD CAMP 2.10 PM handed to DIEFRINGHE where it entrained at 3.55 PM for 'A'(S) FARM. Batt. reached HILL TOP FARM 6.2 PM.	h.S.
HILL TOP FARM	23/11/17		Preparing table shots and Equipment.	h.S.
BELLEVUE AREA	24/11/17		Battalion moved from HILL TOP FARM at 2 W.P.M. FARM. A and B Coys relieved the Support and reserve companies of the 2nd K.O.Y.L.I. C Coy relieved one Coy of the 2nd MIDDLESEX at MUSSELMACK, D Coy relieved one Coy of the 2nd WEST YORKS. Relief reported complete at 7.0 P.M. 4 O.R. wounded.	h.S.
BELLEVUE AREA	25/11/17		A and C Coys withdrew without relief into B and D Coys at dusk. C and A Coy lost heavily owing to a hostile barrage being put down in the front line area.	h.S.

Army Form C. 2118.

WAR DIARY
or
INTELLIGENCE SUMMARY.
(Erase heading not required.)

Instructions regarding War Diaries and Intelligence Summaries are contained in F. S. Regs., Part II. and the Staff Manual respectively. Title pages will be prepared in manuscript.

Place	Date	Hour	Summary of Events and Information	Remarks and references to Appendices
BELLEVUE AREA	25/11/17		Battalion was relieved by the 15th H.L.I. Relief complete reported at 11.30 p.m. The Battalion then moved to relieve the 17th H.L.I. in the left subsector via KRONPRINZ FARM. Relief completed 2.0 A.M. 26.11.17. Capt Benson M.C. wounded, 2/Lt McDonald J.R. wounded. 2/Lt Duncan wounded. 12 O.R. killed, 35 O.R. wounded, 7 O.R. missing.	h.S. h.S. h.S.
ESTROSEBEEKE	26/11/17		Held Twr. line. Situation quiet. 2 O.R. missing.	h.S.
LEFT SUB-SECTOR	27/11/17		Situation quiet. Battalion relieved in the left subsector by 1/6 LANCASHIRE FUS. B Coy captured one prisoner on night of 26-27. 8 O.R. wounded. Relief completed by 8.0 P.M. Battalion moved to HILL TOP FARM and complete in hutsby 12 midnight. 1 O.R. killed 2 O.R. missing.	h.S. h.S.
HILL TOP FARM	28/11/17		Preparing battle equipment and stores.	h.S.
HILL TOP FARM	29/11/17		Preparing battle stores and equipment. Enemy shelled the camp with 4.2 shrapnel from 7.0 am - 9.30 am at 6 shells a minute. 2 O.R. wounded.	h.S.
HURST FARM	30/11/17		Battalion left HILL TOP FARM at 7.40 P.M. for HURST FARM. Complete in camp 10.30 P.M. Hostile artillery quiet.	

1/Lt Twerd
W/ Lt Col.
XI Battn R.S.

CONFIDENTIAL

War Diary
of
11th Border Regiment
from 1st to 31st December 1914
(Volume No 25)

Army Form C. 2118.

WAR DIARY
or
INTELLIGENCE SUMMARY.
(Erase heading not required.)

Instructions regarding War Diaries and Intelligence Summaries are contained in F. S. Regs., Part II. and the Staff Manual respectively. Title pages will be prepared in manuscript.

Place	Date	Hour	Summary of Events and Information	Remarks and references to Appendices

Place	Date	Summary	Reference
WESTROOSEBEEK	2.12.17	forming up positions the tape prior to the attack	W.D.
AREA		The Battalion made a night attack on the German positions South of WESTROSEBEEK in conjunction with neighbouring units of 97th Infantry Bde and 2 units of 96th Infantry Bde. Zero hour 1.55 am. The battalion took its objectives but the two leap-frogging Bns fell back before dawn into subsidiary objectives which were held all day until the enemy launched a counter attack at 4.30 pm. Battalion fell back into the old line	
WESTROOSEBEEK AREA	3.12.17	Activity normal throughout the day on both sides. The battalion was relieved at midnight by the 5/6 Royal Scots 14th Infantry Brigade. Casualties for the whole action were Capt J.Bruce killed Capt A.S.Sanderson killed Capt R.M.Mackie killed 2/Lt Richardson killed 2/Lt I.M Jamie wounded 2/Lt Fulton, 2/Lt Ritchie, N. Capt Holman w. 2/Lt Mullyharton w. 2/Lt Ridway kicking 2/Lt McDuff killed w/p Duff w. 2/Lt Abbey w. The Battalion moved from the line to HILL TOP FARM where the tops was given its showers	W.S.
BRAKE CAMP	4.12.17	at ST JEAN STN for DIRTY BUCKET CORNER at 9.30 am arriving BRAKE CAMP 12 noon Company commanders	W.S.
BRAKE CAMP AREA		Reorganisation	W.S.
BRAKE CAMP	5.12.17	Cmp at disposal of Coy commanders	W.S.
BRAKE CAMP	6.12.17	Cmp at disposal of Coy commanders	W.S.
BRAKE CAMP	7.12.17	Cmp at disposal of Coy commanders	W.S.

Army Form C. 2118.

WAR DIARY
or
INTELLIGENCE SUMMARY.
(Erase heading not required.)

Instructions regarding War Diaries and Intelligence Summaries are contained in F. S. Regs., Part II. and the Staff Manual respectively. Title pages will be prepared in manuscript.

Place	Date	Hour	Summary of Events and Information	Remarks and references to Appendices
BRAKE CAMP	8-12-17		Camp at disposal of my ams. Brig. Gen. C.A. Blacklock D.S.O. addressed The Battalion at 10.0 am.	W.S.
DAMBRE CAMP	9-12-17		The Battalion moved from BRAKE CAMP to DAMBRE CAMP at 11.0 am arriving 1.0 P.M.	W.S.
DAMBRE CAMP	10-12-17		Battalion training	W.S.
DAMBRE CAMP	11-12-17		Battalion training	W.S.
DAMBRE CAMP	12-12-17		Battalion training	W.S.
DAMBRE CAMP	13-12-17		Battalion training	W.S.
DAMBRE CAMP	14-12-17		Battalion training	W.S.
DEMBRE CAMP	15-12-17		Battalion training	W.S.
DAMBRE CAMP	16-12-17		Church parade during morning - reorganization and completing of equipment during afternoon	W.S.
DAMBRE CAMP	17-12-17		Battalion moved to WURST FARM by train leaving TROIS TOURS at 2 p.m., arrived WURST FARM 4 p.m., relieved 2nd Bn., Inniskilling Inone.	W.S.
WURST FARM	18-12-17		Battalion on Working parties etc, casualties 2 O.R. W.	W.S.
WURST FARM	19-12-17		Battalion on Working parties etc.	W.S.
WURST FARM	20-12-17		Battalion moved into front line and relieved 14th Bn. H.L.I., relief quiet and complete at 12 midnight, casualties 4 O.R.W.	W.S.

(A7292) Wt. W12859/M1293. 75,000. 1/17. D. D. & L., Ltd. Forms/C2118/14

Army Form C. 2118.

WAR DIARY
or
INTELLIGENCE SUMMARY.
(Erase heading not required.)

Instructions regarding War Diaries and Intelligence Summaries are contained in F. S. Regs., Part II. and the Staff Manual respectively. Title pages will be prepared in manuscript.

Place	Date	Hour	Summary of Events and Information	Remarks and references to Appendices
in the Line	21/12/19		Situation quiet	A.S.
in the Line	22/12/19		Situation quiet. Capt. Cook Gray, M.C. killed	A.S.
in the Line	23/12/19		Situation quiet. 2/Lt. McKinlay wounded. Battalion relieved by 2nd Bn. Manchester Regt. Relief complete at 11 p.m. Battalion on relief proceeded to WINNIPEG and entrained for TROIS TOURS, where battalion detrained and marched to SIEGE CAMP. Battalion present in huts by 5 a.m. 24/12/19	A.S.
Siege Camp	24/12/19		Battalion cleaning up, etc. Coys at disposal of Coy Commanders during morning. Battalion attended Burial Service of 2/Lt. J. Cook Gray, M.C., during afternoon	A.S. A.S.
Siege Camp	25/12/19			
Siege Camp	26/12/19		Physical training & musketry during morning, remainder of day Coys at disposal of Coy Commanders	A.S.
Siege Camp	27/12/19		Battalion bathed during morning, remainder of day Coys at disposal of Coy Commanders	A.S.
Siege Camp	28/12/19		Battalion training	A.S.
Siege Camp	29/12/19		3 Coys on working parties in forward area, remaining Coy improving & cleaning Camp	A.S.
Siege Camp	30/12/19		Battalion entrained at ENVERDINGHE and detrained at AUDRICQ and then proceeded by march route to TOURNEHEM arriving 1 a.m. 31/12/19	A.S.
Tournehem	31/12/19		Coys at disposal of Coy Commanders. Cleaning of billets and reconnoitring training grounds	A.S.

H. Arthur
Lt Col
11th Bn Scottish Rifles

War Diary
of
11th Border Regiment
From 1st to 31st January 1918.
(Volume No. 26)

CONFIDENTI[AL]

Army Form C. 2118.

WAR DIARY
or
INTELLIGENCE SUMMARY.

(Erase heading not required.)

Instructions regarding War Diaries and Intelligence Summaries are contained in F. S. Regs., Part II. and the Staff Manual respectively. Title pages will be prepared in manuscript.

Place	Date	Hour	Summary of Events and Information	Remarks and references to Appendices

2353 Wt. W3141/1454 700,000 5/15 D. D. & L. A.D.S.S./Forms/C. 2118.

Instructions regarding War Diaries and Intelligence
Summaries are contained in F. S. Regs., Part II.
and the Staff Manual respectively. Title pages
will be prepared in manuscript.

INTELLIGENCE SUMMARY.

(Erase heading not required.)

Place	Date	Hour	Summary of Events and Information	Remarks and references to Appendices
TOURNEHEM	1/1/18	10pm	During morning ½ hour P.T. by each Coy, remainder of day Coys at disposal of Coy Commanders	2%
TOURNEHEM	2/1/18	10pm	Battalion and specialist training carried out	2%
TOURNEHEM	3/1/18	10pm	Brigade holiday	2%
TOURNEHEM	4/1/18	10pm	Battalion and specialist training during morning. Recreation during afternoon	2%
TOURNEHEM	5/1/18	10pm	do do do do	2%
TOURNEHEM	6/1/18	10pm	Church Services	2%
TOURNEHEM	7/1/18	10pm	Battalion training and inspection by C.O. during morning. Recreation during afternoon	2%
TOURNEHEM	8/1/18	10pm	Battalion preparation for Corps Commanders Inspection. Snowed all day, indoor lectures, inspection by Corps Commander cancelled, owing to inclement weather	2%
TOURNEHEM	9/1/18	10pm	Battalion carried out Defensive training; Lewis Guns on Range	2%
TOURNEHEM	10/1/18	10pm	Battalion carried out Defensive training; special attention being paid to Wiring	2%
TOURNEHEM	11/1/18	10pm	do do do do Lewis Guns on training	2%
TOURNEHEM	12/1/18	10pm	do do do do do	2%
TOURNEHEM	13/1/18	10pm	Church Services	2%
TOURNEHEM	14/1/18	10pm	Battalion paraded as strong as possible and marched to "B" Range, and carried out firing practices	2%

WAR DIARY or INTELLIGENCE SUMMARY

Army Form C. 2118.

Place	Date	Hour	Summary of Events and Information	Remarks and references to Appendices
TOURNEHEM	15/1/18	10am	Battalion paraded on "B" Range and carried out firing practice	296
TOURNEHEM	16/1/18	10am	do do do do (Application of Close & Refined Close)	296
TOURNEHEM	17/1/18	10am	All Officers & N.C.Os (less O.Sh's) paraded at J.33.a.00.00. for marking out Defensive positions, special attention being paid to Outpost Line Defence. O.Sh's for training	296
TOURNEHEM	18/1/18	10am	Battalion paraded to take up positions at J.33.a.00.00., as marked out on 17/1/18	296
TOURNEHEM	19/1/18	10am	All Coys on Range, Transport moved by two road for LANGEMARCK AREA.	296
TOURNEHEM	20/1/18		Battalion left Tournehem at 4.30am and marched to Audruicq, thence by train to ELVERDINGHE where Battalion detrained and marched to CARIBOU CAMP, Battalion all complete in camp by 5.30 pm	296
CARIBOU CAMP	21/1/18	10am	Cleaning and improvement of camp	296
CARIBOU CAMP	22/1/18	10am	Battalion training during morning, and Recreation during afternoon	296
CARIBOU CAMP	23/1/18	10am	Battalion training, C & D Coys reorganised their Coys into 4 Platoons	296
CARIBOU CAMP	24/1/18	10am	Battalion training, A & B Coys reorganised their Coys into 4 Platoons, Battalion also bathed	296
CARIBOU CAMP	25/1/18	10pm	Battalion left for LA BERGERIE CAMP at 11.15am arriving in camp at 2pm	296
LA BERGERIE CAMP	26/1/18	10pm	A & C Coys moved to Wood 16 and TILLEUL WOOD respectively, and relieving 2 Coys of	296

Army Form C. 2118.

WAR DIARY
or
INTELLIGENCE SUMMARY.
(Erase heading not required.)

Instructions regarding War Diaries and Intelligence Summaries are contained in F. S. Regs., Part II. and the Staff Manual respectively. Title pages will be prepared in manuscript.

Place	Date	Hour	Summary of Events and Information	Remarks and references to Appendices
LA BERGERIE CAMP	26/1/18	10pm	of the 8th Battn. Royal Berkshires as Brigade Reserve.	39L
LA BERGERIE CAMP	27/1/18	10pm	A & C Coys moved forward from WOOD 16 and TILLEUL WOOD & relieved the remaining 2 Coys 8th Battn. Royal Berkshires in the front line, B & D Coys left LA BERGERIE Camp & took over the Brigade Reserve positions vacated by A & C Coys, the whole Battalion relief complete by 1 p.m. Night very quiet, Casualties Nil	39L
IN THE LINE	28/1/18	10pm	Own Artillery opened out 11am and strafed the enemy positions with Gasshells for ½ hour, retaliation very slight, remainder of day quiet. Casualties Nil	39L
IN THE LINE	29/1/18	10pm	Quiet, slight shelling round CATINAT. and MONDOVI FARM. Casualties Nil	39L
IN THE LINE	30/1/18	10pm	Quiet, shelling very slight, Casualties Nil	39L
IN THE LINE	31/1/18	10pm	Very Quiet. Casualties Nil.	39L

J S Mawtrew, Major,
Commanding, 11th Border Regt.

Confidential

War Diary
11th Border Regt
1st Feb 1918 — 28th Feb 1918

Volume 25

WM 27

Army Form C. 2118.

WAR DIARY
or
INTELLIGENCE SUMMARY.

(Erase heading not required.)

Instructions regarding War Diaries and Intelligence Summaries are contained in F. S. Regs., Part II. and the Staff Manual respectively. Title pages will be prepared in manuscript.

Place	Date	Hour	Summary of Events and Information	Remarks and references to Appendices

Army Form C. 2118.

WAR DIARY
or
INTELLIGENCE SUMMARY.
(Erase heading not required.)

Instructions regarding War Diaries and Intelligence Summaries are contained in F. S. Regs., Part II and the Staff Manual respectively. Title pages will be prepared in manuscript.

1st Bn Border Regt

Place	Date	Hour	Summary of Events and Information	Remarks and references to Appendices
	FEBRUARY			
In the field	1st Friday		"B" in the line on right of Belgeane. Outpost line consists of series of posts. By day no movement possible in forward area. By night all men possible work on wire, improving posts etc. remainder carry food and material.	J.R.M.72.
Elifield	2nd Sat.		"B" relieved last night by 1st Dorsets. Relief complete about 11.30 p.m. B" moved into BOSINGE Camp. No work. General cleaning up and parade for foot treatment.	J.R.M.72
Bosinge				
do.	3rd Sunday		Church Parade & baths for 2 B's.	J.R.M.72
do.	4th		Baths 2 B's. "B" moved forward into the line and relieved 1st Dorsets in the same sector as before.	J.R.M.72
In the field	5th Mon.		Sector has been quiet. Wiring carried on by night very difficult as nights are so dark. Patrolling also very difficult on account of darkness and bad condition of ground	J.R.M.72
do	6th Tues		Enemy more active with artillery & M.G's. C.Coy relieved left Coy of 2nd K.O.Y.L.I. Three Coys now in line C, B + D	J.R.M.72
do	7th Wed.		Sector quiet as usual. Hot meals served at night. Frank Pook killed.	J.R.M.72
do	8th Thurs		Everything quiet by day time. Wiring & working by night. Bat. complimented	J.R.M.72

Army Form C. 2118.

WAR DIARY
or
INTELLIGENCE SUMMARY.
(Erase heading not required.)

11th Border Regt

Place	Date	Hour	Summary of Events and Information	Remarks and references to Appendices
	9th	Fri	by Brig. Gen. Blacklock D.S.O. on improvement in defences generally. Relieved last night by 16th H.L.I. Moved back into Brigade Reserve near Canal Bank. Billets crowded & small. B.H.Q. at Boche X Roads. Day spent in cleaning up & Two	J. Rn. Tu.
do.	10th	Sat.	Corporals Redumen. Large staff of officers & men joined from in 6th bat.	J. Rn. Tu.
do.	11th	Sun.	Lt. Col. Bewsley D.S.O. assumed command of bat. one Major Southern M.C. Corpl. at dis- posal of O.C. Coys. Specialist training. Remainder of bat. went to Reduinum.	J. Rn. Tu.
do.	12th	Mon.	Corps. spent day working in reserve area on M.G. emplacements & shelters. Ret unopposed. J. Rn. Tu. Saw one spec. day, camp working round Kleme Area. Billet improved. Lewis	J. Rn. Tu.
do.	13th	Tue.	Gunners, signallers & bombers on specialist training. A repetition of the last two days. Men work about six hours per day while	J. Rn. Tu.
do.	14th	Wed	specialists continue training. Another day's head work on fortifications in the neighbourhood of our billets. Common on Wood & Lanier Farm.	J. Rn. Tu.
do.	15th	Thurs	Very little doing during day. At night Corps working improved area, building posts. Carrying trades & wiring. Specialists carrying on training.	J. Rn. Tu.
do.	16th	Fri.	W where parties by night as usual. Cleaning up & hot inspections by day. Rest up to op.m.	J. Rn. Tu.

Army Form C. 2118.

WAR DIARY
or
INTELLIGENCE SUMMARY.
(Erase heading not required.)

11th Border Regt

Place	Date	Hour	Summary of Events and Information	Remarks and references to Appendices
ct Jul O	17th		ISLAND - VICTORY Roads. Specialist training as usual. B Coy went to Rehearsing in morning. By night all Coys worked on forward area under C.R.E. except 60 men of C. Coy who had 2 volunteered for raid tomorrow night. Capt ROSS., two other officers + 60 O.R. patrolled area over which the Rob. to raid tomorrow	J R M Te
do.	18th		Nothing done all day except specialist training. At night raiding party of 2 Officers ? 2 M.O. Macrae + Lt. Donald., + 60 other ranks of C Coy, carried out raid on enemy posts in three parties. Zero hour 11 P.M. Heavy artillery barrage for eight minutes to prepare way to advance. Right + Left Parties reached objective + found it at 150 yds. behind enemy front system. Centre party unfortunately struck M.G. uncut left by barrage, + had two casualties. 8/M. Macrae killed. + 1 Sgt wounded. Results :- 12 of the enemy ascertained to be dead, one M.G. brought in + patrol of action, one wounded prisoner brought in - Capt. Ross on was later killed for his body of 7/M. Macrae	J R M Te J R M T
JOESTON	19th		Relieved by 1st Borders. Batt left Chesterton + Rd. by train at 3:30 & 10 P.M.	J R M'T
JOESTON	20th		Moved to VANDAMME CAMP near WOESTON. Relief complete 12 noon. Day spent in clearing up, movement of billets, Camp unsettled, consisting of old billets a few huts.	J R M'9

2353 Wt. W2514/1454 700,000 5/15 D. D. & L. A.D.S.S./Forms/C. 2118.

Army Form C. 2118.

WAR DIARY
or
INTELLIGENCE SUMMARY.
(Erase heading not required.)

11th Border Regt

Place	Date	Hour	Summary of Events and Information	Remarks and references to Appendices
OESTON	21st		Coys spent day working in Battle Zone, leaving by trains at 6:45 & 9:15 A.M. Took over 4 A.A. Lewis Gun positions. Coys started in accustomed manhood.	J.R.N.T.R.
OESTON	22nd		Coys again working on Army Line under R.E.; afternoon fatigues & working parties between. Specialist training as usual.	J.R.N.T.R.
OESTON	23rd		Some a gala day. Bn on working bill on railways, shelters, etc. Specialist training as usual.	J.R.N.T.R.
OESTON	24th		Church Parade as usual. Londoners etc returned via Ravaron. Numbers been called returned and went with 2nd Borders to watch cricket.	J.R.N.T.R.
OESTON	26th		Coys at disposal of Coy Commanders for musketry, working, Lewis Gun training. Bn. played 10th A.I.S.H.W football & rugby, won pool.	J.R.N.T.R.
OESTON	26th		Coys working again in battle zone. Officers accounted this hot when we were verifying camp H.Q's. Specialists as usual.	J.R.N.T.R.
OESTON	27th		A repetition of yesterday, coys left Livingston siding by train earlier in the morning. Specialists as usual.	J.R.N.T.R.
OESTON	28th		Bn. workup again in battle zone under C.R.E. Specialists as usual.	J.R.N.T.R.

R.H. Beasley Lt Col
11. Border Regt

WAR DIARY or INTELLIGENCE SUMMARY

Army Form C. 2118.

11 Border Regt 92/3/21 Vol 28

Place	Date	Hour	Summary of Events and Information	Remarks and references to Appendices
ESTON	1/3/1918		Coys disposed of O.C. Coys for training on the range, and in open fighting, signalling, snipers, scouts, Lewis Gunners carry on independently. Lecture in advance to N.C.O.s.	J.R.W.
(ORANGE CAMP)	2/3/1918		Same as yesterday. Training from 9-12:30. Cotranne fatigue leave for trenches. Officers conference. Voluntary Church Service. Preparations before going into line. Relieved 15 L.F. in WORSTON trenches, right sector of CARPENTRIE. No. 1	J.R.W.
do.	3/3/1918		Bde. line consisting of posts extending from 00:10 M30 HD to 19 J00 at U55 B&2. A+D Coys in line, B in support, Quiet, except for M.G. on track by night. T.M.s in OWL'S WOOD. B.H.Q. in CALEDONIA CLUB. Officers patrols covered wire H.Q.	J.R.W.
"	4/3/1918		Artillery active in VELDHOEK-GARRETTA. B Coy moves with C Coy in N. B. and D Coys hold line in depth. C/on reserve.	J.R.W.
do	5/3/1918		B, A and D Coys each have 6 posts of 1 NCO and 6 men + 2 posts in main line. Wiring and working by night.	J.R.W.
do	6/3/18		Quiet except for artillery on main line posts. No movement possible in front owing to enemy.	J.R.W.
do	7/3/18		Artillery active in AJAX MD, SUEZ, VELDHOEK. Relieved at night by 10th A+S.H. relief complete 11:9 P.M. Bat moves to B5 R1 WOOD, into Bde Reserve.	J.R.W.
do	8/3/18		Bat. turned to about 8 A.M. in consequence of raid on A+S.H. about OWL'S WOOD. 2 Coys moves to VIII J End R1 PT. W.M. preacher ran... about 4 A.M. Preparations foreseen forward...	J.R.W.
do	9/3/18		Day of usual preparations + conference. Received 11th R.S. in No.2 tab sector of No.2 802. 7.15 a.m. (ie on stg... on Rd line). B+D Coys hold line of posts from near TURENNE CROSSING to C 10 30 30.	J.R.W.
do	10/11/3/18		Listening Post in front of A Post worked at 1 A.M. two men captured + wounded. Enemy quiet by day. M.G. active by night. Enemy A Post Section 16 of 2 reached the rear near unloaded 15 Posts. Covered by M.G. barrage, they escaped...	5:15

WAR DIARY
or
INTELLIGENCE SUMMARY.

(Erase heading not required.)

Army Form

Instructions regarding War Diaries and Intelligence Summaries are contained in F.S. Regs., Part II. and the Staff Manual respectively. Title pages will be prepared in manuscript.

Place	Date	Hour	Summary of Events and Information	Remarks and references to Appendices
Cherfund	10/11/18		Colony 4 prisoners, Germans reported with Swiss Slavs.	J.P.W.U
do	11.3.18		Enemy quiet by day, active patrols all night. His bn Nr 3 officers patrols left posts 16, 8.11 proceeding along the roads + obtained useful information regarding enemy wire – H.Q.S. Aeroplanes active. Wiring by night.	J.P.W.U
do	12.3.18		Artillery activity abnormal. Enemy shelled E.5, PT.7, AJAX HQ, and Sw. at Cherr al steb. 11. Patrols by enemy active by night. 2 officers patrols left posts 11, 17, & 19 no particle information. Another officers patrol left posts, proceeded along railway + obtained useful intelligence.	J.P.M.U.
do	13.3.18		Quiet day. Enemy put down a heavy T.M. + M.G. barrage on EGYPT No. + Fresh line of posts from COLOMBO to night left at 7.30 P.M. A party of the enemy attempted to rush our posts between dawn and 8 by L.G. and rifle fire. Posts 17, 18 + 19 were heavily shelled. None of the raiders reached our casualties. 2 M.G.s 6 O.R.s 2 wounded / 1 wounded.	J.P.W.U
do	13/14.3.18		Relieved by 10th A.I.H. Relief complete 1 A.M. Battalion moved into Bde. Reserve with HQ at La Chavatiere + Coys in billets.	J.P.W.U J.P.M.B.
Bde Reserve	14.3.18		Men resting by day, working on Army Zone by night.	
do	15.3.18		Two Coys billeted during day. Coys + 2 workings on Army Zone, working parties on ...	

2353 Wt. W2514/1454 700,000 5/15 D.D.&L. A.D.S.S./Forms/C. 2118.

WAR DIARY or INTELLIGENCE SUMMARY

Army Form C. 2118.

Place	Date	Hour	Summary of Events and Information	Remarks and references to Appendices
Bde Res	15.3.18		called, owing to heavy bombardment on No 1 Bde front at 9 P.M. SOS was put up near COLOMBO HO + LITTLEIM stands. This precaution was cancelled at 10.5 P.M.	J R 9 74
do.	16.3.18		Two Coys worked on Corps line by day, the other two Coys during afternoon worked on Corps line near NEY FARM by night. Conferences held concerning proposed raid.	J R 9 98
do.	17.3.18		Then resting by day & preparing tomorrow night. The line again 4 Officers & 60 O.R. chosen to carry out raid in the near future. These details moved to AGRI WOOD at 5 P.M.	J R 9 92
do.	17/18.3.18		Bn relieved 10A & 5H in No 1 Bn sector of No 1 Bde. Relief complete 11.15 P.M. Raiding Officers did patrols over the area to be covered by raiders.	J R 9 74
In the Line	18.3.18		Quiet except for T.M.s around EGYPT HO. & M.G. fire in tracks by night. A & D Coys held outpost line from near TURENNE CROSSING to COLOMBO HO. C Coy in support & B in reserve. Each post to hold 1 N.C.O + 6 men. No movement by day. Wiring & working by night. Half food carried up tomorrow nightly to all posts by B Coy.	J R 9 74
do.	19.3.18		Quiet. No wiring carried by night. Patrol encountered proved in W 6 b & V 12 a between posts 15 & 17. Aircraft active.	J R 9 74
do.	20.3.18		Hostile artillery active around EGYPT HO. Road service cut at 11 P.M. on enemy posts in V 12 a by 3 Officers and 7/Ws Hawk, Oliver + Godwin + 60 O.R. Party was hundred into	

Army Form C. 2118.

WAR DIARY
or
INTELLIGENCE SUMMARY.
(Erase heading not required.)

Instructions regarding War Diaries and Intelligence Summaries are contained in F. S. Regs., Part II. and the Staff Manual respectively. Title pages will be prepared in manuscript.

Place	Date	Hour	Summary of Events and Information	Remarks and references to Appendices
ltaline	21.3.18		3 sections each of 2 O.R. & 1 Offr. Ronders advanced under heavy barrage, but met with stubborn M.G. resistance. They pushed forward to within bombing distance of the M.G.s which were neutralised by barrage, but had to withdraw after accounting for a few of the enemy. Casualties, 1 Offr., 2/Lt R. Gilmour, 1 O.R. wounded in memory, 1 O.R. killed. G.O.R. wounded.	J R M T D
	22.3.18		Quiet except for gas bombardments of both areas. Bn. relieved in line by 16th H.L.I. of 14th Bde. Relief complete 10.30 P.M. Bn. marched back to CANAL BANK. Bde. moved into Div. Reserve. Renders under 2/Lt J.R. McDONALD M.C. rejoined rest of Battalion.	J R M T D
N. RES. NAL BANK	23.3.18		Day spent in cleaning up after tour in line. Bath concentrated in shelters along Canal Bank. 1 Coy after working party in afternoon. 2 Coys billed during afternoon.	J R M D
do	23.3.18		Two Coys on ranges. One Coy bathing & one on working party.	
do	24.3.18		Church Parades in BOSINGHE CHURCH HUT. Warning of more shelling in neighby hills.	
do	25.3.18		Training recommenced. Coys disposed of O.i.C. Coys afterwards detailed. 1 Coy working.	
QUESTN.	26.3.18		Left Canal Bank at 4.30 A.M., entrained at ELVERDINGHE about 11 A.M. & detrained at AUBIGNY at 9 P.M.	

2353 Wt. W2514/1454 700,000 5/15 D. D. & L. A.D.S.S./Forms/C. 2118.

WAR DIARY or INTELLIGENCE SUMMARY

Army Form C. 2118.

(Erase heading not required.)

Instructions regarding War Diaries and Intelligence Summaries are contained in F. S. Regs., Part II. and the Staff Manual respectively. Title pages will be prepared in manuscript.

Place	Date	Hour	Summary of Events and Information	Remarks and references to Appendices
	26/3/18		Bn. Transport left by road ok 12 noon. Marched to WANQUETIN arriving dark 9 miles during an aerial bomb (indiscriminate) escaped.	JR9710
BANSART	27/3/18		Battle stores issued before leaving from Cinema Barn. Resolving morning. Practised attack on flanks. Available nightly to RANSART, where battalion arrived in sundries routes till morning.	JR9710
In field	28/3/18		Battn. moved at 9.30 a.m. to occupy old trench in vicinity of (ADINFER WOOD, 2 coys in reserve & 2 coys in support. Later in day rear companies to fall back hearing attack in Alcohol of C.O. Weather: B.M.O in rear.	JR9710
	29/3/18		Bde in reserve to Brigade Division. Bn. moved forward into gulley & road Zouaves enforced.	JR9210
do	30/3/18		Bde relieved by 96th Bde late by 10th L.F. Relief complete 10.30 p.m. Bn moved forward when advanced position reached by the Somewhat Scots. Infantry of MOYENVILLE to AYETTE.	JR9110
do	31/3/18		B & C Coys bivouaced in Aus reserve. H.Q. in entrenchment near Quiet except for aeroplane & m/g at night. An enemy plane bombed local steam laughs enemy. 2 dark prisoners of war registrant arrived	JR9210

R. L. Beazley, LtCol
Commanding 11th Border Regt.
31/3/18

WAR DIARY or INTELLIGENCE SUMMARY

Army Form C. 2118

11 Border Regt

Vol 29

Place	Date	Hour	Summary of Events and Information	Remarks and references to Appendices
In the Line 25.d.9.1 & 27.d.0.0	1st Apl		The Battalion is at present Nos. 2 Bn of Nos. 3 Bde & holding the line in front of MOYENNE VILLE & COURCELLES. D, B & C Coys in the front line; each Bn do approximately 300x; having 3-5 outposts such a length of old Sunken Track behind to accommodate their support. A Coy in reserve along sunken road 300x behind front line. B.H.Q. in entrenchment at X.19.d.5.8. Day quiet except for shelling around Sugar factory in X.19.b. Enemy planes active. Wiring by night. Wounded prisoner captured by B Coy & numerous identifications brought in from dead Germans.	
do	2nd Apl		Heavy shelling of C Coy's line causing a few casualties. Day otherwise quiet. Snipers very active, numerous hits observed. Aeroplanes active. Patrols report on reviewing enemy posts. A Coy relieved C Coy in the left Coy sector & C moved into Reserve. Wiring by night. Enemy reported massing in front of B Coy. Later 500-600 seen leaving trench behind front trench in small parties; there were probably reinforcements made up to hold & repulsed attack. Situation normal again at 11 A.M. Day quiet. Advance parties of A & S.H. arrive. Guns reconnoitre purple line. Batt. relieved by 10th A & S.H. Relief completed at 11.20 P.M. Moved back to PURPLE LINE with H.Q. in ADINFER.	
do	3rd Apl			
PURPLE LINE	4th Apl		B, C & D Coys in trenches in purple line F.26.9.1 to X.22.d.0.0. A Coy in shelters on northern side of ADINFER. Day well spent in improving trenches & shelters. Wiring by night.	
do	5th Apl		Another miserable day. Trenches in bad condition. Shelling of valley in X.27.b. Wiring by night.	
do	6th Apl		Weather brighter. Germans seen up & chance to recuperate after long spell in the line. Officer's bath arrives. The new sector ADINFER heavily shelled & whose huts.	

WAR DIARY or INTELLIGENCE SUMMARY

Army Form C. 2118

Instructions regarding War Diaries and Intelligence Summaries are contained in F.S. Regs., Part II. and the Staff Manual respectively. Title Pages will be prepared in manuscript.

(Erase heading not required.)

Place	Date	Hour	Summary of Events and Information	Remarks and references to Appendices
PURPLE LINE.	7th Apr.		Day quiet. Advance parties proceed to take over from 4/K.O.Y.L.I. in No.1 sector of Nr.3 Brigade. Transport heavily shelled at BIENVILLERS, 2 civilians and 1 O.R. wounded. Batt. relieved 4/K.O.Y.L.I. in right sector of Bde. A&B Coys in line, C in support + D in reserve. H.Q. in old German dugout at X.29.6.9.8. Relief complete 10.30 P.M.	
The Line 16.a.45 to 25.d.9.1.	8th Apr.		Line held similarly to left sector. Right Coy. has 4 posts and 200+ out of front and left. Coy has 5 posts + a similar length of trench. Working head during whole time, morning in fronting posts by night, sitting old Boche wire by day + waiting machines for own enemy attack any time. Day quiet. Patrolled night located several enemy posts.	
do.	9th Apr.		Enemy patrol surprised outside our wire at 6 A.M. in the morning, and fired on. Party retired, but sent on again + gave themselves up. 10th A&S.H. got 7 prisoners in ref X.29.c.0.7. Hostile Artillery active on COEUL VALLEY. B.H.Q. moved into new dugout in tanks + roads. Patrol located enemy	
do.	10th Apr.		Day quiet. Enemy appears to be repairing and reconstructing posts in A.2.c. Local reliefs. Moved from O.P. at A.1.a. 20.8.5. 90 evils of wire put out by self.	
do.	11th Apr.		Day quiet except for shelling of front line shortly after dawn. Protective + reconnoitring patrols were all as usual in the early morning. From O.P. movement marching was seen in enemy outposts at A.1.c. d., A.8.a+b, round MOYENVILLE + along the roads opposite on front. D Coy relieved A Coy + C Coy relieved B Coy. C Coy old positions in support was abandoned. B Coy occupied old german positions + Arty moved into Bde. Reserve in creek in X.2.8.b. + dug themselves in.	

WAR DIARY or INTELLIGENCE SUMMARY

Army Form C. 2118

Place	Date	Hour	Summary of Events and Information	Remarks and references to Appendices
[...] Line	12th Apr.		Artillery active on both sides. Much enemy movement seen & various posts & trenches reported to Bde. & Artillery. Aeroplanes – rather active. Usual patrols running by night.	
do.	13th Apr.		Visibility poor, and little activity on either side. Enemy occupied by day battling in Green Hub, carrying forward material & reinforcing shelters. Little enemy night activity. Intense darkness. A Coy commenced wiring in front of their reserve posts.	
do.	14th Apr.		Gun artillery very active. Enemy sniped slightly & fired shots at enemy posts. Slight retaliation. Visibility good and various posts & party of enemy reported wiring.	
do.	15th Apr.		Artillery active on both sides. Posts at F12d central & F18b central reported & fired on by artillery. Patrols active as usual. Enemy continued at night. Coys continued battling. Wiring artillery.	
do.	16th Apr.		Visibility poor. Day quiet. Bn. Reserve Coy. dug fire position in front of Rue bank. Advance party of A&S H. arrived & arranged for relief.	
do.	16/17 Apr.		10th A&S.H. relieved Batn in line + on completion at 10.30 p.m. we moved back into Bde. reserve.	
Bde. Res.	17th Apr.		H.Q., C&D Coys in trenches & dugouts at RABBIT WOOD. B Coy in PURPLE LINE + A Coy with Bde. between MONCHY & BERLES AU BOIS. Coys resting & cleaning up. Batn in reserve ready to man PURPLE LINE in case enemy attack. O.R. established at WINEFER [?]	
	18th Apr.		Coys for training under Coy. arrangements. Rain interfered. Battling commenced at MONCHY.	

WAR DIARY or INTELLIGENCE SUMMARY

Army Form C. 2118

Place	Date	Hour	Summary of Events and Information	Remarks and references to Appendices
Rec	18th Apr		There was strenuous shelling & but stores were quickly carried up & no shelling.	
do	19th Apr		Leave as yesterday. Coys at disposal of O.C.'s for training, but rain largely interfered. Battn.	
do	20th		Day spent quietly in preparation for going into the line tonight. Officers reconnoitred line. No shelling. Battalion finished bathing at MONCHY.	
le Line	20/21st		Battn relieved 2nd K.O.Y.L.I. in the left subsector, A & B Coys going into front line, D into Support & C into Reserve. Relief complete at 10.30 P.M.	
	21st Apr		Battn. holding line from S.26.c.1.1. to S.27.a.0.0., comprising 11 outposts + 10 piquets. Enemy quiet, but aircraft active. Own patrols were very active by night. Inward & Reserve Coys moved very little by day but stood the night ready to support Coys engaged in carrying. Enemy quiet by day, W. reconnoissance about by day in the distance. Own patrols turning features actively by night.	
	22nd		Heavy shelling of Sugar Factory in X.19.a., day otherwise quiet. Enemy found close to No.10 Post. B. brought C & D relieved B + A Coys. respectively.	
	23rd		Hostile Artillery more active by day. Attempted raid on enemy post in front of 20.10. failed because Stokes Barrage overshot the post & enemy saw the party in the moonlight. Preparations for relief. Events reconnoitred line. Enemy quiet. Levels relieved	
	24th			
	25th 25/26th		on completion at 12.10 A.M., battalion marched back to RANSART – MONCHY road & embussed for LAHERTY, arriving about 4 A.M.	

Army Form C. 2118

WAR DIARY or INTELLIGENCE SUMMARY

(Erase heading not required.)

Place	Date	Hour	Summary of Events and Information	Remarks and references to Appendices
HERTIE	26th		Reveillé 12 noon. Battalion billeted in scattered village about 10 miles from the line via At. I have nothing to move. Men are billeted in barns etc, officers in houses. Day spent cleaning up, reclothing & refixing deficiencies. Assembly for the remainder of training commenced. Both rounds from 9 A.M. to 10 A.M. boys at disposal of O.C. thereafter during afternoon. Football competition arranged.	
do	27th			
do	28th		Church Parade for Brigade held at La Bazèque Farm at 11 A.m. thereafter the whole Brigade marched past the G.O.C. The battalion leading. The afternoon and evening saw the first round of the football competition decided, and the four teams of our battalion all lost.	
do	29th		Battalion parade from 9am to 10am, thereafter company training same as the 27th. Lectures held at 7-30 p.m. on 13 lay killed.	
do	30th		Battalion and Company training same as yesterday.	

R.S. Beazley Lt Col.
Commanding 11. Border Regt

APPENDICES.

SECRET   Ref. No. G. 3/5/1

Instructions for 97th Infantry Brigade when in RESERVE.

Reference Sheets 51.C and 57.D. 1/20,000

1. Position of Our own Troops.
   (a) The VI Corps Front is held as follows :-

       Right Division Sector   ... Guards Division.
       Centre Division Sector ... 2nd Division.
       Left Division Sector.   ... 2nd Canadian Division.

       Division in Third Army Reserve
       (at disposal of VI Corps in
       case of attack) ... 32nd Division.

   A tracing showing the Divisional boundaries and lines of Defence in the Corps Area is attached.

   (b) The French 129th Division has two battalions accommodated one at BIENVILLERS and one at BERLES-AU-BOIS.

   In case of attack these Battalions will occupy the RED Line from 1st junction with the MONCHY SWITCH (E.4.c.0.0.) to Point 147 (inclusive) xxxxxxxxxxxxxxxxxx xxxxxxxx about W.17.a.0.0. with Posts pushed out along the MONCHY SWITCH to MONCHY (inclusive) and thence North to Point 147 in selected portion of the old British and German Lines.

   Note :- Each French Battalion has a M.G. Company and in addition a Field Company is attached to it.

2. Role of Reserve Division.
   The 32nd Division is to be prepared for any of the following tasks :-

   (a) To Counter-attack to regain the PURPLE LINE if penetrated on any part of the VI Corps front as far North as ADINFER VILLAGE SPUR.

   (b) To occupy if requierd :-
      (i) The front line of the Third System RED Line from the BIENVILLERS-AU-BOIS - FONQUEVILLERS Road to its junction with the MONCHY SWITCH.

     (ii) The old British Line from E.16.d.3.0. to the MONCHY SWITHC (E.12.c.)

    (iii) The old German trenches in E.12.c. and a.

    (iv) The MONCHY SWITCH from its junction with any of the lines indicated above to its junction with the PURPLE RESERVE Line in X.25.b.

     (v) The PURPLE RESERVE LINE from HAMEAU to the MILL in X.8.d.

3. Most important Tactical Points.
   With reference to para. 2(a).
   The most important tactical points which must be regained by counter attack if lost are as follows :-
      (i) SAUSAGE RISE and QUESNOY FARM.
     (ii) The old British trenches in E.16.d. & E.11.c.& a.
    (iii) The old german trenches in E.12.c.& a. & E.11.b.
    (iv) MONCHY SWITCH in E.6.c. &a W.30.d. & X.25.c.
     (v) HAMEAU FARM Plateau.
    (vi) ADINFER VILLAGE SPUR.

/4.

=2=.

4. Rendezvous in Case of Attack.

Brigades will be prepared to move immediately to the following RENDEZVOUS on receipt of orders from Divisional H.Q. :-

A. 97th Inf. Bde. - Valley S.W. of BERLES -AU-
   (Right Brigade)   BOIS in W.26.b.
                     Bde.H.Q. - HUMBERCAMP.

B. 14th Inf. Bde. - Valley N.E. of BERLES - AU
   (Centre Brigade) BOIS in W.10.c. and d.
                     Bde.H.Q. - BAILLEULMONT.

C. 96th Inf. Bde. - Valley S.W. of MONCHIET in
   (Left Brigade).   Q.26.c.
                     Bde H.Q. - GOUY CHATEAU.

The above rendezvous will be known by the letters A, B and C respectively.

5. Movements of 97th Inf. Bde.

97th Inf. Bde. (Right Bde.) will be prepared to move as follows :-

(a) 10th A.&.S.Highrs. (No.1 Bn)
1 Company to Outpost position in old British line E.16.d. and E.17.a.
Battalion H.Q. and 3 Companies to hold RED line and MONCHY SWITCH from BIENVILLERS - FONQUE - VILLERS Road (inclusive) to point where HANNES-CAMP-MONCHY ROAD Crosses MONCHY SWITCH at E.10.b.5.8. (inclusive).

(b) 2nd K.O.Y.L.I. (No.2 Bn.)
1 Compnay to Outpost position in old German line E.12.a. and c. and E.6.d.
Battalion H.Q. and 3 Companies to hold MONCHY SWITCH from left of 10th A.&.S.highrs. to point where MONCHY SWITCH crosses MONCHY - QUESNOY Road E.6.c.

(c) 11th Border Regt. (No.3 Bn.).
Will be in Brigade Reserve at the Rendezvous A. (Valley S.W. of BERLES in W.26.b.).

(d) O.C. 97th T.M.B. will place one section (2 Mortars) at disposal of each front line Bn. and will retain two sections in Reserve at Rendezvous A.

(e) O.C. Company 32nd Bn. M.G.C. now at BEINVILLERS will allot one section each to No.1 and No.2 Bns. and will join Brigade Reserve at Rendezvous A. with remainder of his Coy.
O.C. Nos 1 and 2 Bns. will allot 1 sub-section each to their outpost Company.

(f) L.G. Limbers, Medical carts and pack animals will accompany units.
Brigade S.A.A Reserve will move to covered position in V.23.a. just N. of GAUDIEMPRE - CAUCHIE Road.
Brigade Transport (1st Line) will move to triangular clearing N. of BAZEQUE FARM in V.15.d.

(g) Communication by Visual, Runner and all other available means will be established.

(h) Brigade Headquarters will be on E. edge of HUMBERCAMP in V.29.b.

(i) The positions taken up by Nos. 1 and 2 Bns. will also include the defence of the E.15. E.16., E.17., E.11. and E.12 squares and close touch must be obtained and maintained with neighbouring bodies and these Bns. must be prepared for all eventualities and if necessary to form defensive flanks

= 3 =

6. Movements of 14th Inf. Bde.

14th Inf. Bde. (Centre Bde.)

The 14th Inf. Bde. will be prepared on receipt of orders from the Divisional Headquarters to move as under :-

(a) Two Companies to move direct to Outpost positions in the MONCHY SWITCH from the MONCHY - QUESNOY Road to its junction with the PURPLE RESERVE.
(b) 14th Inf. Bde. (less 2 Companies) from rendezvous position :-
 (i) To the Valley in W.23.a. and W.17.d.
 (ii) To occupy the MONCHY SWITCH from its junction with the QUESNOY - MONCHY Road to its junction with the PURPLE RESERVE Line in X.26.b. and the PURPLE RESERVE LINE in X.26.b. Northward to the MILL in X.8.d.

<u>Note</u>:- Outpost Companies indicated in paras 5 and 6 will push out patrols and keep in touch with the situation to the front and flanks.

7. Movements of 96th Inf. Bde.

96th Infantry Brigade (Left Bde.).

The 96th Inf. Bde. will be prepared on receipt of orders from Divisional Headquarters to move from rendezvous positions as under :-

(a) To occupy the RED line from BASSEUX Northwards to VI Corps boundary in R.9. central.
(b) To move South in reserve to the other two Bdes.

8. Reconnaissance.

Reconnaissance for the action laid down in para. 5 will be carried out <u>at once</u> and O.C. Units will submit their general dispositions to Bde. H.Q. by 9.p.m. 27th April.

O.C. 97th T.M. Battery and M.G. Coy. will get into touch at once with their affiliated Bns. and carry out the reconnaissance with them.

O.C. No.3 Battalion will reconnoitre this area.

<u>In addition</u>.

O.C. Units will at the same time reconnoitre generally the area FONQUEVILLERS - ESSARTS - WESTERN Edge of ADINFER WOOD.

Special attention should be paid to the contingency of a counter-attack being necessary to regain QUESNOY & ESSARTS RIDGE

(a) With ESSARTS ours.
(b) With ESSARTS in enemy's hands.

9. A C K N O W L E D G E.

J.E.Laurie.
Capt.
Brigade Major.
97th Inf. Bde.

25th April.1918.

Copies to :-
 11th Border Regt.
 2nd K.O.Y.L.I.
 10th A.& S.Highrs.
 97th T.M.Bty.
 32nd Bn.M.G.C.

9. While in 3rd army Res ready at one hour's notice to move from 8 am to 12 noon & 2½ hours notice from 12 noon to 8 am. (BM of 26th inst)

A move
B
C delt
D

A ____ ACTION
B. guns   9⎞
C. MG   ⎟92
D. [sig]   ⎠

Please read
& pass in above
order quickly
A Coy & return [sig]

[sig]

(1086) Wt.W1650
Form C2122 (of 150)

Prefix	Code	Words	At........m. At........m.
Office of Origin and Service Instructions.			From... To...
			By... By...

TO

PREFIX	~~PRINT.~~	~~POWER~~	PROCTER.
		~~PUSH~~	~~CRUSH~~

Sender's Number.	Day of Month.	In reply to Number.	AAA
B.M.1.	26		
Reference	this	Office	G3/5/1.
of	25th.	inst.	AAA.
Cancel	para.	9	and
add	AAA	while	in
Third	Army	Reserve	Units
of	97th.	Inf.	Bde.
will	be	at	one
hours	notice	to	move
from	8. a.m.	to	12 noon
and	2½	hours	notice
from	12	noon	to
8 a.m.	AAA	ACKNOWLEDGE.	
			J.G. Lavoie
			Capt

From			
Place			
Time			

* This line should be erased if not required.

SECRET.   Ref. No. G.

11th Border Regt.
2nd K.O.Y.L.I.
10th A.& S.Highrs.
97th T.M.B.
Brigade Transport Officer.

        In order to be prepared to move in case of alarm <u>as ordered</u> the following precautions will be taken by units:-

1. Units will always leave their billets in complete fighting order ready to move off <u>without returning</u>.
    To effect this O.C. Units will make what arrangements they think fit with regard to their surplus baggage etc.

2. Units will train within a 2 mile radius of their billets and the most adequate means of communication must be maintained in order to give the alarm at once.

3. No Officer, or man will leave his billeting area without permission of this O.C., who will ensure that he can be recalled at once. Leave other than of a very local character, will be granted in special cases only.

4. The Brigade Transport Officer will ensure that the Brigade Transport is ready to move as ordered within the time limits laid down.

5. In the case of Brigade exercises, the same precautions exist but the responsibility rests with the Brigadier.

6. In case of reconnaissance only a proportion of the officers and N.C.Os. dhould be away together. The exact number is left to the O.C. Units but they will ensure that their units have orders as to their action in case of alarm, and that the Officer left behind in Command is fully conversant with these.

7. It is most important that each unit should notify Brigade Headquarters with the locality in which they are training. This will be sent without fail by 5.p.m. each evening for the following day.

                                                Capt.
                                      Brigade Major.
                                      97th Inf. Bde.

25th April. 1918.

Secret B.M.1   Copy

To 97th Inf Bde

Reference Para 5 of your G 3/5/1 of 25th April 1915
The 11th Bn. The Border Regt in Brigade Reserve
will be formed up in two lines. Two
Companies in first line and two Companies
in second line behind crest of hill.
Each Coy in artillery formations by platoons
at 40 yds intervals.

Fifty yards distance between 1st + 2nd lines

```
         <————————————— 300x —————————————>
 |<40x>|  |   |   |   |   |   |   |   |
         ~~~~~~ No 2 Coy  ~~~~~~ No 1 Coy
 |50x|    ~~~~~~ No 4 Coy  ~~~~~~ No 3 Coy
 |<40x>|  |   |   |   |   |   |   |   |
```

27. 4. 15.   R L Beasley Lt Col.
                                    11. Border Regt

Ref. No. G. 3/5/3

11th Border Regt.
2nd K.O.Y.L.I.
10th A.&.S.Highrs.
97th T.M.B.
Officer i/c Brigade S.A.A. Reserve.
32nd Division (for information).

      Reference Instructions for 97th Inf. Bde. when in Reserve this office No.G.3/5/1 dated 28th April sub-para (f) of para 5 is cancelled and the following subsitituted :-

(f) (i) Lewis Gun Limbers, Pack Animals and the Maltease Cart will accompany Battalions to the RENDEZVOUS at W.26.b.

    (ii) The Brigade S.A.A. Reserve will assemble at V.23.a 3.6. just S. of the GAUDIEMPRE - LA CAUCHIE Road where it will be marshalled by the Officer i/c Brigade Reserve (2/Lieut. COLOMBO, 11th Border Regt.) and will then follow 11th Border Regt to the RENDEZVOUS.

    (iii) The remainder of the Regimental 1st Line Transport will assemble at V.17.c.8.3. when it will be marshalled by the Brigade Transport Officer and will then follow the Brigade S.A.A. Reserve to the RENDEZVOUS.

David Kiddie
Capt.
Brigade Major.
97th Inf. Bde.

30th April.1918.

CONFIDENTIAL

39 Div / 32

WAR DIARY

OF

11TH BORDER REGT.

From May 1st To May 31st
1918

VOLUME

Vol. 33

Place	Date	Hour	Summary of Events and Information	Remarks and references to Appendices
HERLIERE	1st May		Battalion and Company training carried out	
Do.	2nd		Battalion and Company training during forenoon, night operations from 8 P.M. to 11.30 P.M.	
Do.	3rd		Forenoon spent preparing to move. Battalion moved from La Herliere at 2 P.M. Arrived 4 P.M. billets in Lavans etc.	
LRES-AU-BOIS	4th		Usual company training during forenoon, afternoon devoted to recreation, football, boxing etc.	
Do.	5th		Church parade at 10 A.M.	
Do.	6th		Usual company training during forenoon, recreation athletics in	

Lt.Col. Tuohy		Usual company training during forenoon. In the afternoon at Beaucourt ribbon for military services to 2/Lt J Short and Bar to DSO to Lt Col Bisley, presented by corps General, also DCM to L/Cpl Todd
Do	8th	Usual company training and afternoon recreation
Do	9th	Usual company training and sports, at mid-night this Bn. will cease to be known as 11th Border Regt. and are now 1/5th Border Regt. Strength 173 O.R's Junior 10 officers and 173 O.R's. Junior Capt. J.M. Fagan. Capt S. Hack. Lieut Col Bickley. 2/Lt W.N Marks 2/Lt F.J. Poolson. 2/Lt I. Cahone. 2/Lt I. S. Haynes 2/Lt O.E. Knight. 2/Lt A.B. Tolleron. 2/Lt G. MacKenzie. Lieut A. MacKenzie 2/Lt 11th Border Regt.

Signed A. Hart on behalf. 11th Border Regt.

WAR DIARY

MAY 1918 — 11th Bn. The Border Regt.

Army Form C. 2118.

INTELLIGENCE SUMMARY

Place	Date	Hour	Summary of Events and Information	Remarks and references to Appendices
L'ARBRET			Out at midnight of 9/10 May the 5th & 11th Bns. The Border Regt. were amalgamated and after amalgamation a Training Cadre of 10 officers & 51 O.R. was formed and designated 11th Bn the Border Regt.	
	12 May		Remained roll of Cadre to stand. The Cadre left 32nd Division and proceeded from LA FEUQUIÈRES to join 66th Division.	
	13 May		The Cadre arrived FEUQUIÈRES and marched to billets in MAISNIÈRES.	
	14-19 May		Spent in training the Cadre in train entrainment & waiting for 328 U.S. Inf. Regt. to arrive & Battalion 2nd Bn the Border Regt. O.C. 11th Bn The Border Regt.	

Army Form C. 2118.

11th Bn. R.E. Fusiliers Regt.

WAR DIARY
or
INTELLIGENCE SUMMARY.
(Erase heading not required)

Place	Date	Hour	Summary of Events and Information	Remarks and references to Appendices
	13/19 May		The 11th Bn. R.E. Fusiliers Regt. was under administration of 198 Inf. Brigade but on 20th May was transferred to 199 Inf. Brigade.	
	20 May		The 11th Battn. 328 O.R. Inf. Regt. arrived & was united to Coy B VIGNY & Coy B V.R. with the M.G. Coy at HOCQUELUS.	
	22 May		The Colonel moved to BUIGNY. Training commenced and continued daily. In very fine weather. TILLOY & MONTIERES & MONTCELET entire canvas.	

Lt. Colonel Co-d.
O.C. 11th Bn R.E. Fus. Regt.

Army Form C. 2118.

(3)

WAR DIARY
or
INTELLIGENCE SUMMARY

(Erase heading not required.)

71" Bn. The Border Regt

Place	Date	Hour	Summary of Events and Information	Remarks and references to Appendices
	29		Inspection of 1st Battln 328 U.S. Infantry Regt at work in conjunction with Cadre of 11 Bn by General PERSHING — Training order emphasises an attack by Field Marshall Sir Douglas HAIG	
	30		The training to form practically one of all arms of Branches of Personnel together — Lewis Guns — nonnewering & firing Field work (Demonstration) Demonstration & Practical Stokes order drill demonstration. Platoon 2.5" Pr Progress satisfactory. En. Coldill Lt.Col O.C. " Bn The Border Regt	

-CONFIDENTIAL-

39 Div
32

WAR DIARY

OF

11ᵀᴴ BORDER REGᵀ

FROM :- June 1ˢᵀ 1918   TO :- June 30ᵀᴴ 1918.

VOL Nº

June 1918

WAR DIARY 11th Bn. Rl Border Regt.

Army Form C. 2118.

INTELLIGENCE SUMMARY.

(Erase heading not required)

Place	Date	Hour	Summary of Events and Information	Remarks and references to Appendices
	1 June		The Battn. moved from BUSNY (Gommiers) and MONTHELET to PENDE. Superiority Reg (Gommiers) 1st Battn 328. 1 Coy who proceeded to SELLENELLE to 320 ammunition M.G. Battn. returning 2/7th Londoners Regt Coy Coms 1 Coy was moved to ESTREBOEUF & 320 ammunition M.G. Coy. Training continued.	
	5 June		1 Coy who were requested Bath Coms at PENDE was relieved by 2/7th Bn Londoners returning Coy Coms. Training continued in previous matters & good manoeuvre.	
	16 June		Inspection made 328 Regt Regt left for onto...	

OC 11th Bn R Border Regt

Army Form C. 2118.

WAR DIARY 1/1 Bn. 72 Border Regt.
or
INTELLIGENCE SUMMARY.

Place	Date	Hour	Summary of Events and Information	Remarks and references to Appendices
PENDÉ	16/18 June		Cadre continued its own training - refresher courses &c	
	18 June		2nd Lt. Tn. 108 American Inf. Regt. 27th American Div. 4 officers & 2 coy comdrs. proceeded to MONS-BOUBERT to begin training.	
	19 June		The Cadre divided. 3rd Lt. Tn. 108 American Inf. Regt. to FRANLEU & 3rd Bn. 105 American Inf. Regt. 27th American Div. 4 officers & 2 coy comdrs. to MIANNAY to 2 Lt. Tn. 105 Inf. Regt. Training proceeded.	
	22 June		The Cadre proceeded by march route to DOULLENS stopping at on pullarens – in glorious weather.	

E. Lebel Lt Col
OC 1/1 Bn 72 Border Regt

WAR DIARY 1st Bn. The Border Regt.
INTELLIGENCE SUMMARY

Place	Date	Hour	Summary of Events and Information	Remarks and references to Appendices
			Night of 22/23 June - 169. & 2 Coys ONEUX 2 Coys COULOUVILLERS HEUZECOURT LE MEILLARD	
	23/6/24		-	
	24 June		Marching with 3rd & 4th Bn. 105 Inf Regt. respectively arrived DOULLENS - billets in town	
	25/26 -		Training continued - weather good -	
	27 June		The whole Corps left DOULLENS and marched to AILLY WHOM CLOCHER and reorganised night of	
	27/28		at BERNAVILLE - AILLY WHOM CLOCHER arrived AILLY WHOM CLOCHER	
	28 June		Bn. H.Q. and 1st Bn. Tn. 130 & organised 33rd American Division by Regt.	
	29 June		Training commenced.	Sd. W. Ashill LtCol OC 1st Bn. The Border Regt.

Infantry Regt. (American)
1 cy Ceder Jourded to SELLENELLE G 320
American M.G. Party G 320
G Ceder. 1 cy Ceder moved to ESTREBEUX
G 320 American M.9. cy

5 Jun Training continued
        1 cy Coffee established
        Roughly Invalid — L.9. dgar
        Battle Hdrs at HENDE
        Kneif retained by 2/7 - 7th Lancashire Fusiliers
        coy Caderes.

16 Jun Training continued in glorious weather & great
        Improvement made.
        328 Regt. left the area —
        O.C. II = 7th Lt Col. E. Sclwell L.Col.
                             7/7 Bradford Regt.

WAR DIARY 1/1st 72 Brigade 7 Army

Instructions regarding War Diaries and Intelligence Summaries are contained in F.S. Regs., Part II. and the Staff Manual respectively. Title pages will be prepared in manuscript.

Army Form C. 2118.

INTELLIGENCE SUMMARY.
(Erase heading not required.)

Place	Date	Hour	Summary of Events and Information	Remarks and references to Appendices
TENDE	16/1/18		Coys continued to run Gunning - refresher courses &c.	
	18 June		2nd Bn. 10th American Inf. Regt. arrived. 4 officers & 2 Coy Cadres proceeded to Mons-Boubert with Comdg of 34 Bn. 10th American Inf. Regt.	
	19 June		The Cadre under G FRANLEU & 34 Robb 105 American Inf. Regt. 4 officers & 2 Coy Cadres to MIANNAY G 2nd Bn. 105 Inf. Regt. Training proceeded.	
	22 June		The Cadre provided by British unit in glorious weather marched into DOULLENS & stagung on to Corbie —	

E. Lollwheel
O.C. 11th N.L. Border Regt.

Army Form C. 2118.

WAR DIARY
or
INTELLIGENCE SUMMARY.

(Erase heading not required.)

1/1 Mr. The Border Regt

Place	Date	Hour	Summary of Events and Information	Remarks and references to Appendices
	22/23 Jne		Nights of 22/23 Jne – 169 & 2 Coys ONEUX 2 Coys COULOUVILLERS HEUZECOURT LE MEILLARD	
	23/24			
	24 Jne		Marching with 34 & Lt. M. Gs & 5 Jy Regt regards. Owned DOULLENS – billets in the town.	
	25/26		Training continued – weather good.	
	27 Jne		The Batta came up to DOULLENS and marched to AILLY à Haut CLOCHER stopping right of	
	27/28		at BERNAVILLE.	
	28 Jne		Owned AILLY à Haut CLOCHER. 26/4 H Brigade Batta R.A. 1/30 33rd American Division	
	29 Jne		Training [inserted]	In the field Col OC 1/1 M. The Border

CONFIDENTIAL.
_____

WAR DIARY

OF

11th Batt. Border Regt.

From 1st July 1918   To 31st July 1918

(VOLUME.....).

==========================

WAR DIARY
INTELLIGENCE SUMMARY

July 1918 — 11th Bn. N. Border Regt.

Army Form C. 2118.

Place	Date	Hour	Summary of Events and Information	Remarks and references to Appendices
AILLY LE HAUT CLOCHER	1st July		Training 1st Batt. 130th Inf. U.S.A.	
	18 July			
	20th		Moved to EPAGNE	
EPAGNE	21st		Received orders to move to ABANCOURT — see orders ann.	
	22nd		Entrained for ABANCOURT at 6 p.m.	
ABANCOURT	23rd		Arrived ABANCOURT 1 a.m. Marched to camp.	
"	24th		Orders received for 11th Bde. N.B.R. to be disbanded and for personnel to be posted to the B.E.F. (90 G.H.Q. 7137 A).	

En. [signature] Lt. Col.

Army Form C. 2118.

July 1918   WAR DIARY 1/11th Bn. The Border Regt.
or
INTELLIGENCE SUMMARY.

(Erase heading not required.)

Instructions regarding War Diaries and Intelligence Summaries are contained in F. S. Regs., Part II. and the Staff Manual respectively. Title pages will be prepared in manuscript.

Place	Date	Hour	Summary of Events and Information	Remarks and references to Appendices
ABANCOURT	26.		Orders for disbandment of 11th Batt. Border cancelled. (196 Suffolk 17379. 297/10)	
	29.		Training	
	29th		Orders received for H.Q. N.C.O.'s men of the 11th to proceed to join the 1/5 Batt. Border Regt. E.A.S. letter C.A. S/9054/20.F.) 11th Battalion to be disbanded from 29/8/16 of Sparker.	appendix I.
	30.			
	31st		11th Batt. Border Regt. ceased to be 10.3 am this from remescamp to join 1/5-Bn. Border Regt. 11th Batt Border Regt. disbanded from today.	

Jn. Laird Lt Col
O.C. 11/2 Bn The Border Regt.

Appendix I.

COPY.

C.R. S/9084/

G.O.C.,
L. of C. Area.

With reference to O.B./2231 dated 16.7.1918 :-

(1) Please despatch personnel (W.Os., N.C.Os. and men) of the
Training Staffs named below, up to Establishment laid down O.B.
dated 11.4.1918, and as amended by O.B./1851/A dated 27.4.1918
Units shown. Any surplus personnel belonging to such battali
sent to their respective Base Depots.
Orders regarding officers will be issued by A.G., G.H.Q.

Battalion Training Staff :-

11th Border Regt.   to join 1/5th Border Regt.

(2) Nominal rolls of personnel proceeding either to units or t
Depots, as above, should accompany them (stating any special qu
they may possess - and in the case of W.Os. and N.C.Os. their
rank), copies being sent to this office; number and date of t
should be quoted on the rolls.

(3) The number of W.Os., N.C.Os. and men comprising the Battalion
Training Staffs and date of departure from 66th Division should be wired
to Headquarters of the Formation to which they are proceeding, and
repeated to this office - such date to be taken as the date of disbandment
of the Battalions to which the Training Staffs belonged and the W.Os. and
N.C.Os. concerned will revert to their permanent rank from that date.

Copy of instructions as to disposal of these battalions Training
Staffs on arrival with their new units is attached for your information.

(Sgd) EDW. Graham,
Major General,
Deputy Adjutant General.

G.H.Q.,
3rd Echelon,
26th July, 1918.